Y0-DXB-305

TYPES OF SOCIETY IN MEDIEVAL LITERATURE

TYPES OF SOCIETY
IN
MEDIEVAL LITERATURE

By
FREDERICK TUPPER

BIBLO and TANNEN
NEW YORK
1 9 6 8

Originally published 1926

Reprinted, 1968

by

Biblo and Tannen Booksellers and Publishers, Inc.
63 Fourth Avenue   New York, N.Y. 10003

Library of Congress Catalog Card Number: 67-29555

Printed in U.S.A. by
NOBLE OFFSET PRINTERS, INC.
NEW YORK 3, N. Y.

CONTENTS

TYPES OF SOCIETY
IN MEDIEVAL LITERATURE

I

CONDITIONS OF MEN

Your Colver lecturer of this year has more than once asked himself whether his topic, "Types of Society in Medieval Literature," will carry even to a university audience aught either of charm or of challenge. How win attention and good will through anything seemingly so alien to your present interest? The very word, "medieval," so doubtful in both spelling and pronunciation that we know not the long or the short of it, commonly conveys a suggestion of the outworn and obsolete, unless straightway coupled with architecture in its glory or with education in its power. The modern misses in the Middle Ages the whir of the machine, "the snorting steam and piston stroke;" the classicist, secure in his own perfect, has paid—until his recent impressive invasion of late Latinity—small heed to the subtle lure of the imperfect. The medieval, too, has been corrupted, it appears, by the evil communication of that monster of frightful mien, the academic, and hence connotes to many only collations, reprints, theses, grammars and lexicons. Scholarly attempts to bring back the medieval mastodon long since evoked Carlyle's tremendous yawn of protest:—"Alas, what mountains of dead ashes, wreck and burnt bones, does assiduous pedantry dig up from the Past Time and name History and Philosophy of History, till, as we say, the human soul sinks wearied and bewildered; till the Past Time seems all one incredible gray void without sun, stars, hearth-fire or candle-light!"

That eloquent boredom was but the expression of an everyday impatience with the medieval world. A misty, mid-region of weariness, darkened by Pangloss and Dryasdust! Now this sweeping indictment against the scholarly study of the so-called "Dark Ages" of Aquinas, Dante, St. Francis, Roger Bacon, has been gallantly refuted by the lyrical enthusiasm of the newly created "Medieval Academy of America." The charge will serve us now simply as a preface to two markedly contrasting points of view. Our modern age, in its sophistication, deems the past—particularly the past of its own language and literature—so remote that it will not link the life of the Middle Ages with its hurrying world of thought and speech and action. Our strong sense of difference breeds indifference. On the other hand, the Middle Ages, in their nearsightedness, looked at yesterday through the eyes of to-day and, in their abysmal ignorance of historical perspective and local color, imparted even to the centuries of Greece and Rome the form and hues of their own modernity. What was of their age was of all time. "There is no new guise that is not old." The medieval mind, quite unable to fancy another situation from that in which it stood, thus brought the past up to date, and made light the labor of historian and poet. The chorus of responsible reviewers rises sharp and shrill when Tennyson's *Idylls of the King* (or of the "Prince Consort," if you wish) image King Arthur as a modern gentleman. Was Malory a whit more accurate in clinging close to the conception of the medieval knight? But the difference between the two anachronisms is significant. That of the nineteenth-century poet is an artistic perversion, which no man accepted; that of the fifteenth-century romancer is a time-honored tradition which no man questioned. When Cleopatra treads our stage as a vivid flapper, Helen as a model housewife, Hamlet in a dinner coat, we applaud or hiss the *coup de théâtre*. Five hundred years since, the Queens of Egypt and of Troy were deemed neither more nor less modern than the Prince of Denmark or the Maid of Orleans. Chivalric romance bestows its accolade upon Joshua and Solomon, Hector and Alexander, breaks lances in tourney at ancient Athens and canonizes Venus and Lucretia; while sober history places the crowns of the Henries and Edwards upon the brows of scores of shadowy British Kings. Time was, time is, time shall be, untouched by the changes that wreck single lives.

If the past was deemed like the present in form and fashion, it was admittedly superior in tone and temper. Medieval man with damnable iteration chants paeans over the bygone and dirges over the now. To him nothing seemed as good as it used to be. Exaltation of the golden age, poetized by ancient Ovid, philosophized by modern Rousseau, leads inevitably in Boëthius, Jean de Meung and Chaucer to disparagement of their own hour, full of avarice, duplicity, treason and murder. And the conventional praise of primitive life was no stronger than the constant idealization of the past of history. Dead days were always tinted with *couleur de rose*—what ought to be under the false semblance of what was. Guiot de Provins, French moralist of the early thirteenth century, mourns with transcendental disregard of chronology that the spacious and beautiful times of Arthur, Alexander, Cæsar, Ahasuerus and Frederick Barbarossa have shrunk to the nothingness of the pitiful present. "All is lost," he cries, as he bewails the passing of the generous kings and captains of his youth. Ichabod! Ichabod! Contempt for the contemporary inspires a hundred satirists. Of course the golden glow of yesterday fades into common day, as we turn back the page. "Notable miracle!" exclaims shrewd Walter Map a generation earlier. "The dead live, the living are buried in their stead. The illustrious deeds of modern men of might are little valued and the castaway odds and ends of antiquity are exalted. No one speaketh of living Cæsars." He adds that, "in every century its own present hath been unpopular and each age from the beginning hath preferred the past to itself—hence my own times have despised me. My only fault is that I am alive." Our latter age has changed all that. The last great English writer of romance anent the Middle Ages, Charles Reade, vows never again to attempt a story like *The Cloister and the Hearth*. "I write for the public, and the public don't care about the dead. They are more interested in the great tragi-comedy of humanity that environs them at every

crossing, in every hole and every corner."
In our self-absorption and self-sufficiency
we taint with reproach the very names of
past periods, whether near or distant.
"Victorian" and "medieval" are alike
anathema. Contempt for the "ante-
diluvian" supersedes the exaltation of
"the giant race before the flood." We
open our purses to the antique, but our
prejudices to the ancient.

Medieval discontent with the present,
the abiding conviction that whatever is,
is wrong, finds hissing vent in three com-
prehensive accusations of society. First,
all sorts and conditions of men are weighed
in the balance by the contemporary
critic, and each class or profession is
found wanting in the essential virtues of
its type. Kings have forgotten how to
rule, lords to give, knights to defend,
clerks to pray, peasants to labor. All are
degenerate. Secondly, the evil that is
everywhere abroad in the world assumes
hellish shapes of sin, as lurid as the cloven-
hoofed, forked-tailed Lucifer of old belief.
Pride, the acknowledged lord of France,
has married off three of his daughters in

England—Envy, Luxury, Drunkenness. "Manners, virtue, freedom, power," all have yielded to the sway of these and other deadly vices. Thirdly, womanhood has fallen from grace and is no longer the theme of honor's tongue. Late espoused saints seem now less common than early unespoused sinners. These three motives (themes of our three lectures)—the external orders, the infernal fellowship, the eternal womanly—sometimes diverse, often meeting and mating, are the constant themes of the student of medieval society; and satire is wontedly the song. Thus may we gain some insight into standards and ideals.

Our immediate concern is not merely with medieval points of view, but with the imaginative expression of these in literature. Authorship of the past, which displays so many contrasts with authorship of the present, is nowhere more at variance than in its attitude to the property rights of the creative artist. This difference may be fittingly shadowed forth by the Old English distinction between *bōcland* and *folcland*. To-day the writer's

ground is *bōcland* or bookland, a private
estate or preserve inclosed within the
fences of charters and copyrights and
guarded against trespassers and poachers
by all the signs and mantraps and air-
guns of the law. In the yesterday of
the Middle Ages literary territory was
land of the folk, property of the commu-
nity—as open as Hampstead Heath, not
a warning notice anywhere! Over this
broad common moralist or romancer
might range at will, without feeling of
encroachment, or fear of constable, taking his own wherever he found it. If
aught of value came to him from another's
thought and pen, or better still from the
minds of many others, he shouted it
perhaps for the hundredth time, in as-
sured confidence in its value. Where
all was "free and general as the casing
air," no sense of obligation oppressed
the medieval mind. The word fitly spoken
was sanctified by such constant repetition
that it became a formula, dear through
its very familiarity. Literary traditions
abounded. For generations men ran
through the same bits of song about

the glory of yesterday and the shame of
to-day, the classes of society, the duties of
kings and of knights, the branches of
sins, the precepts of love, the perversi-
ties of women, with occasional varia-
tions of the old, old tunes, to which we
must listen if we would read the times
aright. God made medieval man up-
right, but he found out many conventions,
rather than inventions. Indeed the old
was so much weightier than the new, that
even men of genius were wont to give the
spurious authority of age to their freshest
creations and to their latest borrowings
from their fellows by assigning these to
ancient writers real or fictitious. Chaucer's attribution of a fire-gilt tale of
his own to one Corinne and his citation
of an unknown Lollius instead of Boccaccio as the source of *Troilus* will be
remembered. Medieval literature is com-
munal, conservative and conventional.

Large confidence in conventions ac-
companied a childlike faith in generaliza-
tions. It was surely no man of the
Middle Ages, who declared, "All general-
izations are untrue"—and then added,

"including this one." Universal was the
delight in sweeping conclusions anent
the world and its people. Careless of
the single life, medieval society was ever
careful of the type, perhaps because all
forms and functions seemed rooted in
the eternal order of things. In the medieval world class categories and characteristics were inventoried and tabulated
beyond our conception. It has been truly
said that "medieval political speculation
is imbued to the marrow with the idea
of a structure of society based upon
distinct orders. The idea of an estate
extends to every social function, to every
profession, to every group" (Huizinga).
On the higher steps of the social edifice
are the representatives of chivalry and
the church, on the lower the thronging
crowds of common folk of every kind.
This earthly hierarchy, like the heavenly,
is fixed by God and no one dares question.
Divisions of medieval society in all its
branches—"which they were, and of what
degree"—confront us in numerous social
satires, in the so-called *états du monde*
in the books of manners, the "mirrors,"

the moral poems, the sermons, the political verses, the chess books, the ships
of fools, the dances of death and in the
poems of Chaucer's chief poetic contemporaries, Gower and Langland. John
Gower, writer in French, Latin and English, and a great gentleman, too, divides
the world into the three conventional
degrees: clergy, knighthood and peasan-
try. In the first estate are mighty prelates of the Court of Rome, cardinals,
bishops, deans and parsons, curates of
parishes, and priests without a cure, the
religious orders—monks and nuns and
mendicant friars; in the second estate,
that of knighthood, are emperors, kings,
lords, knights and men at arms; in the
third estate are not only peasants but
craftsman and merchants. "Spiritual-
ity," "Temporality" and "Merchande,"
are indeed, the names of the classes
in Sir David Lindsay's famous satire.
No distinction is drawn between bourgeois and proletariat. The richest trades-
man is, like the poorest plowman, a
villein, to whom lofty qualities cannot be
ascribed, as they are both of servile

degree. In the dawn of a new day Sir Thomas More reveals his faith in the common people by picturing an ideal state without class distinctions, a government in which the highest offices may be held by ambitious handicraftsmen. But even in the sixteenth century, that was a land of nowhere. In the twelfth Walter Map quotes with equal approval two sayings concerning men of low estate: the verse of Claudian, "Nothing is harder than the lowly whenever he rises to high degree," and the homely English proverb of wide currency, "Take a dog as companion and a stick in thine other hand." Even John Gower, who was not without charity, sees in a popular rising only the rooting of unclean swine, and the raging of untrained dogs. Apparently there is not the slightest recognition of the social power of the people, whose only ideals should be humility and service.

The medieval mind was not content with frequent catalogues of the classes of men; it must also codify meticulously the qualities of each class. Each division of society from king to cook, from

prelate to plowman, has its typical traits.
The literature of the Middle Ages is
expository rather than descriptive, zeal-
ously arraying and illustrating the general
in preference to the particular and individual. The Dutch scholar, Huizinga,
is doubtless right in regarding this mental
tendency as "a result of profound idealism, of the imperious need of always and
especially seeing the general sense, the
connection with the absolute, the moral
ideality, the ultimate significance of
things. What is important is the im-
personal. The mind is not in search of
individual realities, but of modes, examples, norms." In Chaucer's delightful
Prologue are *individualized conventions*
of each class of society. The poet indi-
vidualizes in recalling the scenes of the
Knight's wars, in assigning names to
Host and Prioress, to Reeve and Friar;
in giving to the Shipman a barge, the
Maudelayne, at Dartmouth; he conventionalizes in making the Monk slothful
in good works, the Miller thievish, the
Friar intimate with women, and the
Doctor ignorant of the Bible. We cry

out with delight as some figure stands
forth with all the glow of his own native color, and we chase fatuously the
will-o'-the-wisp of personal identification.
The medieval reader felt doubtless a
far greater satisfaction in the typical
characteristics of each occupation. Chaucer is to us a great portrait-painter; to
his own time a dexterous expositor or
generalizer.

If the interest in the specialized type
is keener than in individuals of the profession or trade, why humanize the figures
by giving them other than type-names?
So doubtless reasoned Chaucer when he
refrained from christening many of his
pilgrims; so, too, those writers of moralities and interludes who, a century later,
presented to an applauding public Taverner and Cook and Pardoner and Friar.
In a more modern time love of class-
traits readily yields to a keen appreciation of personal values, and the so-called
"Characters" of the seventeenth century,
heavy bundles of conventional attributes
often as old as Theophrastus, are happily
succeeded by the vivid personal por-

traits of the life-like representatives of contemporary society that we meet in *The Spectator*. The generic descriptions of the sundry folk of the medieval master give way in his disciple John Masefield's "Reynard the Fox" to sympathetic characterizations of the strongly marked personalities of an English countryside.

The conventions and traditions of medieval orders and estates are nowhere better illustrated than in the moralities of the popular chess books of the period. A more engaging theme than "Chess Moralities and Medieval Conventions" would have been "Chess Mortality and Medieval Unconventions." For, while this ancient and honorable game is deemed by us of to-day a pastime well within the bounds of personal safety, it counted in the Middle Ages almost as heavy a toll of victims as the automobile or aëroplane with us. Alexander Neckham, foster-brother of Richard Cœur de Lion, laments the sudden fits of passion to which the players seemed peculiarly prone, and the brawls into which the game often degenerated. (By the way, the survivor of a victory over Richard must have been Fortune's darling.) Then Neckham bewails the many thousands of souls sent to hell in consequence of that game in which Reginald, the son of Eymund, while playing with a noble knight in the palace of Charles the Great, slew his opponent with one of the chessmen. Indeed, in several of the Charlemagne romances, notably those of "Ogier the Dane" and "Renaud de Montauban," the pieces seem to have been valued as weapons of offense chiefly by their weight as missiles—and the chessboard itself represented the only mode of meeting this very effective line of attack. A contest in which the men were used by one player, the board by the other, was often ended in one move and was never renewed. Nor did ladies soften the game unduly. There was, for instance, that sanguinary checkmate of wife by husband, a ninth-century Breton noble, of which Walter Map tells with especial unction. If you have tears for "unhappy far-off things," you may dry them speedily, for all these encounters of high romance occurred a century or two before chess was introduced into Western Europe. Hence they are no more or less authentic than the medieval tradition that ascribes the invention of the game to a Chaldean sage,—a lover of justice and measure. This worthy's master, a certain King of Babylon, quite as shadowy as he of Henley's poem, was "a jolly man without justice" and so cruel that he caused his father's body to be hewn into three hundred pieces and gave it to eat and devour to three hundred birds that men call vultures. To reprove this particular blend of jollity and injustice, a little too strong even in a king, and to correct the ruler by teaching him self-mastery, apparently somewhat needed, the game of chess was designed by the wise man. This hectic prelude will perhaps reconcile you to the safer if tamer theme of Chess Moralities.

If we may judge from the changing names of the pieces, Chess, in the days of its oriental origins, was simply a picture of war. Later, when it came into

Europe just before and during the Crusades, it seemed to represent, first the organization of a Germanic state, and secondly, the life of all the world—the relation of the various classes of men to each other and to God. Conversely the whole world often appears to the allegorizing medieval mind, as to Omar Khayyam, a game of chess, which the Almighty plays, moving kings, nobles, burgesses and peasants here and there, making them win or lose. The conception of the chess game as a microcosm of society and its different estates owed its wide extension to the vogue of one of the most popular of all medieval books, the *Liber de Moribus Hominum et Officiis Nobilium* of Jacobus de Cessolis, probably a Lombard by birth and certainly a Dominican preacher at Rheims in the late thirteenth century. Meeting the current taste, the Latin *Chess Book* was rapidly borne to the uttermost corners of Europe. It was not only translated into every language but it inspired huge expansions of its theme like that of Kunrat von Ammenhausen, on the Swiss

Rhine near Constance, and suggested sentimental variants like "Les Eschez Amoureux." Its illustrations crept into the great storehouses of medieval legends and *exempla* like the *Gesta Romanorum*. And yet the Latin original was not printed until 1479 in Milan, five years after William Caxton set into type at the town of Bruges his English version of the *Chess Book* derived from De Vignay's French translation of de Cessolis. The popularity which attended all versions of the *Chess Book* and which provoked a second and illustrated edition of Caxton's rendering seven years after the first was due not only to every gentle's liking of the royal game, but to every reader's childlike love of the obvious moral. Old de Cessolis and his crew wrote everywhere across the sixty-four spaces of the board, their morality large.

And so the pieces are placed upon the table. In the rear stand the gentles, first the bailiff or legate of the king, represented by rook or castle, second the knight, third, the judge, denoted by the alphyn (the Persian elephant, our bishop), fourth the queen or fers, fifth the king, and then judge, knight and bailiff again. The pawns, standing in front, symbolize the common people in their various ranks, eight very arbitrary divisions of plain men: first, the field-laborer or farmer; second, the smith of every sort; third, the clerk, be he notary, advocate or scrivener; fourth, the merchant or money-changer; fifth, the physician and the apothecary; sixth, the taverner, hostler or victualler; seventh, guards and custom officers; eighth, ribalds and dice-players. Such a classification as this is in complete accord with the love of categories, the desire to get all things on a list and with the medieval propensity to pass in review the various orders of society—the estates of the world. But the customary divisions of man social differ from the *Chess Book* in this regard, that they are primarily intended to satirize the typical vices of each occupation, whereas de Cessolis and his followers prefer to portray the ideal virtues of the different classes. Nor does the *Chess Book* in its simplest

form give any place to representatives
of the church, who offer so fair a mark
to the slings and arrows of the popular
satirist. But abundant illustration of
the fitting qualities of the other estates
serves as luminous commentary upon
many medieval traditions.

The enumeration of the qualities of
an exemplary king carries us into the
region of royal education, trodden in
widely different ages by a Xenophon and
a Machiavelli, and, more to our immediate
purpose, discloses the same ideals of
kingcraft that are revealed in a dozen
famous tracts and poems of the Middle
Ages. Those who know all the rules of
our game of scholarship and are alive to
the dreadful possibilities of the parallel
column may well cower under the menace of a sustained comparison between
the sovereign qualities of a monarch in
the *Chess Book*, and in John of Salisbury, Egidio Colonna, the *Secretum Secretorum*—and other representatives of
the ethical traditions of Aristotle, some
genuine, some spurious. I shall merci-
fully soften, if not avert the blow, by

hurriedly remarking that the mercy, truth, hatred of cruelty, justice and chastity, befitting the King of de Cessolis, are among the royal virtues of each list. Written large in many medieval categories of royal attributes are the four cardinal virtues of the *Ethics* and *Politics* of Aristotle, traceable through Plato to Socrates, but colored by Christian teaching—Wisdom, Justice, Fortitude and Temperance. Wisdom goeth before the others as director giving the light of counsel and making the King rule by reason in fear of the Lord. Indeed practical wisdom is preëminently *the* royal characteristic. Walter Map's ideal King, Henry I, was attended before luncheon by those ripe in years, so that his court was "a school of virtue and wisdom all the morning." Justice is of the kind and nature of God, and a king in fulfilling that is like unto God; yet royal justice must be seasoned by temperance, or the mercy incarnate in Christ. Portia's famous speech on Mercy, which "becomes the throned monarch better than his crown"—and is "enthroned in the heart of kings" has its roots not only in the Bible and in Seneca, but deep in our medieval traditions. Indeed, before the development of equity, the prerogative of mercy belonged to the King and not to the courts. How this "blesseth him that gives and him that takes" is seen in Map's encomium upon good King Louis of France who enforced his decrees with tears; his sovereign mercy in only cutting off the right ear of an offender is wonderfully betokened by the earlessness of the criminal's posterity. Fortitude, defined as courage or strength, makes a king put himself in peril for things of great price. He must be a strong man, speaking little but to the purpose yet with a voice twice again as loud as another's (Schoolmaster Partridge's idea of a king in *Tom Jones*). Such strength must be blended with meekness, for the stingless king-bee is a model unto princes. The true king should put God's law above his own, and should make himself beloved by his people, while tyrants are not subject to divine law, and despise the commonweal.

The four cardinal virtues are expanded in the *Ethics* to a full dozen. Even Liberality or largesse, so characteristically medieval, finds full warrant in Aristotle's assurance that kings cannot be prodigal, for it does not appear easy to exceed the greatness of their possession. Thomas Hoccleve assures Prince Hal that a foolish largesse beggars a king and curses a people, yet there is a place for wise giving:- "Let *me* stand in your benevolence."

The king-becoming graces of young Malcolm in *Macbeth*,

"As justice, verity, temperance, stableness,
Bounty, perseverance, mercy, lowliness,
Devotion, patience, courage, fortitude"

may be traced back through Holinshed's far shorter lists to the categories of the Middle Ages. A lack of such virtues as these is "the sword of our slain kings" in all the old versions of *The Fall of Princes* from Boccaccio's original down through the various Elizabethan editions of *The Mirror for Magistrates*. Herein all men may read of "the untimely falls of such unfortunate princes and men of note as have happened since the first entrance of Brutus into this island until this, our latter age." The last edition of the *Mirror* (in Joseph Hazlewood's three splendid volumes) was published in 1815, the very year of the downfall of the greatest of princes, Napoleon Bonaparte. All these stories are "tragedies" —as the Middle Ages reckoned tragedy— the sudden fall of men of high estate. The greater the prince and his prosperity, the greater the challenge to Fortune—a dreaded deity in those insecure days when hearts were bowed under much reflection upon the uncertainty of human life and the inconstancy of happiness. Over the unhappy fate of mighty conquerors Fortune laughs and makes sport. Her wheel turneth ever. Her ominous frown falls ever upon a place in the sun. Her unexpected strokes fall heaviest upon kings who are proud, for it is "high pride" (the *hybris* of the Greek, the superhumanity of Nietzche) that she always assails. Hence the discourse of medieval sermonizers upon fallen greatness are brimful of royal examples of punishments

meted out to the deadliest of the sins.
That wonderful legendary, the *Mirror*,
points the moral of retributive justice
in many stories, historically apocryphal
but amazingly apposite in our own generation. Here is the tale of one Guidericius
(perhaps an anticipation of Gulielmus),
who "became desyrous to winne all the
worlde and spoyled France, Germany
and a great part of Italy, yet furnished
by his miserable end a syngular ensample
of God's vengeance against pride and
arrogancy"; and here is recounted (*mir-
abile dictu*) the hapless fall of a king who
"was minded to conquer Britain," but
died wretchedly "in forayne soyle" ex-
horting men to take heed by his folly
and rashness. Not until our own hour
could men forecast the *finis* of the event-
ful history of the fall of princes. Nicholas,
William, Karl, Constantine, Ferdinand,
and the Germanic host of fallen kinglets
and princelings—these crowd the last
lurid pages of a volume which will need
no sequel. Nor do we folk of the twentieth century deem this tremendous finale
a *tragedy*.

The Middle Ages set side by side with *The Fall of Princes* a medley of even deeper wisdom, *The Regement of Princes*, the composite of many manuals for the mental and moral guidance of royal youth. Thomas Hoccleve, the chief of those who turned into English currency this wealth of traditional instruction, admonishes Henry V, Shakespeare's Prince Hal, that a king must above all keep his faith, must hold his word sacred. "The people of Scythia and Arabia were ruined by the falseness of their kings, who misused sworn pledges to deceive neighboring countries and thus broke bonds that had been established for the good of mankind." Of modern peoples and their rulers this story has been told. Had Hoccleve known his own country's literature, he would have added that truth is the very essence of the early Germanic ideal of kingship, citing as evidence the boast of the dying Beowulf: "At home I bided what fate might come, I held my own with justice; I followed no treacherous warfare nor ever swore false oaths." The old poet holds aloft before

Hal the idea of humility—the sovereign
gentleness of Alexander and Scipio, the
gracious meekness of David and Solomon.
By a score of examples the *Regement*
attests that this temperate justice of the
monarch preserves subject peoples from
oppression. Need we pause to seek modern instances in the Near or Middle
East? The soldiery of a merciful prince
will "observe the rights of battle as truly
as the rights of peace, harming no children and helpless folk in captured towns,
but bearing arms only against armed
men." Five centuries later, did mighty
kings and captains thus wage knightly
war?

Hoccleve's manly and pious offset to
The Fall of Princes closes with a spirited
appeal to all Christian rulers for a lasting
peace. "He who maketh strife is a
wretch. Accursed be the greedy heart
that will swallow all, with wrathful will
and crabbed pale face and hostile hand
dealing revengeful stroke! Let peace
drive out strife, friendship banish hate,
tranquillity kill ire!" In this fervent
prayer the Middle Ages found nothing

exceptional or exceptionable. The church
had early been the vehement champion
of peace. And only ten years before,
old John Gower, writing at even greater
length, "In Praise of Peace," had ex-
horted young Henry's father, Henry IV,
just entering upon his reign, never to
shed blood, save in the cause of right-
eousness, for, "if a king truly understood
how great an ill it is to slay the people,
then deadly wars and all their heaviness
would at once cease." The reproach of
the modern "monarch in shining armor"
was not, as some have said, that he
followed medieval ideals but that, in his
glorification of pinchbeck medievalism,
he missed utterly every exalted ideal that
the true Middle Ages cherished.

I have said that "the moralized *Chess
Book* serves as luminous commentary
upon many medieval traditions"—and,
I may now add, upon conventions vivi-
fied by genius, notably those individualized conventions, Chaucer's "Canterbury
Pilgrims." Many of us have been source-
hunters at one time or other, yet few
of us will deny that the literary coinci-

dence is often quite as significant as the direct borrowing. The second means mere reproduction, the first offers adequate testimony to the strength of tradition. Whatever the probabilities, it cannot be demonstrated that Chaucer was immediately indebted to the medieval *Chess Book*. Hence the resemblance between sundry of his motives and those of de Cessolis may well arise from a like origin in the rich soil of contemporary convention.

"At a Knight then will I first begin." He must put chivalry and the church first. The dominant trait of Chaucer's Knight is his "worthiness." No less than five times in twenty-five lines (A 43–68) is he called "worthy." But this adjective, so sweeping in its range, obviously carries a loftier connotation than when applied later in the Prologue to Friar, Merchant, Franklin and Wife of Bath. And more than one editor or translator have rightly interpreted the epithet as implying neither worthiness in the modern sense, nor yet "high social position," but prowess, the chief badge of knighthood. The Knight is a *preu' homme* or brave man. But then comes the puzzling antithesis:—

"Though that he were *worthy*, he was *wis*"

Though there is, as Professor Lounsbury said long ago, "no necessary contrast between courage and wisdom," yet the *Chess Book* brings support that is final to those who would render the line, "Though he was a brave man, he was a prudent one." De Cessolis, the author of our *Chess Book* makes *wisdom* (*sapientia*) the first of the seven traits of his knight, ranking it above fidelity to leaders and companions, liberality, strength, mercy, care of the people and regard for law. And wisdom spells to him the skill and prudence born of long experience in the tented field. Caxton's rendering of the Latin of the *Chess Book* must serve us now:—"A noble knight ought to be *wise* and proved before he be made knight; it behoveth him that he long time used the war and arms, that he may be expert and wise for to govern others. For since a knight is captain of a battle, the life of them that shall be under him lieth in his hand, and it therefore behoveth him to be wise and well advised. For sometimes art, craft and engine is more worth than strength or hardiness of a man." The *Chess Book* adds that youths are never chosen as leaders because there is no certainty of their wisdom, and that Alexander conquered the world more by the counsel of old men (*prudentia*), than by the strength of young men (*fortitudo*). This opposition of *fortitudo* or *audacia*—which Caxton calls "strength or hardiness," and which we term "physical bravery"—to *sapientia* (*ars et prudentia*)—which Caxton variously renders "wisdom, counsel, art, craft and engine,"—is exactly what Chaucer intends to convey. He says of his veteran what Gen. Maurice, the English military expert, says of Marshal Foch (*Fortnightly Review*, January, 1919, p. 34), "Unlike Ludendorff, Foch was prudent as well as daring."

Indeed this distinction between bravery and prudence crystalizes into a medieval formula. Thomas Hoccleve develops it at length in his paraphrase of the *Chess Book* in *The Regement of Princes*. He urges the young Henry to be prudent, for an unwise leader has often ruined an army. He adds that skill in battle is worth more than hardihood (*Id.* 3984f):

"Experience and art in a bataille
 Of the prudent knyght more may profit
 Than hardinesse or force may availle
 Of him that thereof knoweth nought or lite.

       *   *   *   *   *   *   *   *   *   *

 But be a knyght wys or corageous
 Or have hem bothe at ones at his lust,

       *   *   *   *   *   *   *   *   *   *

 On his manhood is ther but litel trust."

Egidio Colonna (*De Regimine Principum*, Pt. III, Bk. II) develops the theory that "those who are born and dwell in warm climates lack hardihood, but are wiser and better advised than the natives of the North, who excel in valor. Only in temperate regions are the two qualities duly mingled." John Barbour, earliest of Scotch poets, taking a leaf out of Aristotle's *Ethics*, asserts that "valour is the mean between foolhardiness and cowardice. Robert Bruce overcame because wit went with his boldness." And many knights of romance mingle worthiness, or hardihood on which all prowess is grounded, and wisdom. Chaucer's Troilus is "a well of worthiness, a wise and worthy wight;" and Sir Guy, Sir Bevis, Sir Degrevant bear a like repute in all Christian and heathen lands that grandiloquent geography can suggest. Indeed the blending of the two qualities antedates chivalry, for the epic hero, Beowulf, is both *snotor* and *swȳthferhth* ("prudent and stout-hearted"). In the significant phrase of the *Chanson de Roland*, "Roland is brave, and Oliver is wise." On their last battlefield at Roncesvalles Oliver thus reproaches his friend: "Comrade, the fault is thine, wise valor is not rashness; and prudence is better than recklessness. Through thine imprudence the French have met their end. Wo worth thy prowess, Roland!" In the French romances, *preux* and *sage* are coupled as often as "worthy" and "wise" in the English. Very much to the purpose is a passage from De Joinville's *History of St. Louis* (295): "The Duke of Burgundy, of whom I have just spoken to you, was a very good knight with his hands, but he was never accounted wise either towards God or towards this world. And because of this the great King Philip said he hoped that God would make the Duke's namesake as valiant (*preux*) a man as the Duke. And they asked him why he had not said, *prud' homme*. 'Because,' said he, 'there is great difference between a valiant man (*preu' homme*) and a *prud' homme*.'" Chaucer's Knight is the ideal knight of the *Chess Book*. Like Bruce and Oliver he combines wisdom with his bravery. He is not merely a *preu' homme* but a *prud' homme*.

> "Such is he
> That every man at arms would wish to be."

The knight's sovereign price is no less dependent upon his worthiness than upon his liberality, freedom, largesse. He must be free of hand, large in giving, so that the heralds, the press agents of that day, will publish abroad his deeds—crying, "Valiant, valiant, lo wherever he goes!" —and fame of his prowess will come to his lady's ears. The rule of largesse, extolled as the queen of medieval virtues, often degenerated into tyranny. There was Henry the Liberal, Count of Champagne, so prodigal that he gave to every man that asked of him. And there was the genially irresponsible young Lothario of thirteenth-century romance, Joufroi of Poitiers, who, arriving in England, won all men's esteem by lavishing upon poor knights jewels, cloaks, arms and horses, and who later rid himself in the twinkling of an eye both of King Henry's gift of seven hundred marks, and of his bourgeois bride's dowry of a thousand more. This freedom of dispense seemed even then a trifle overdone. Good old Gower in his *Mirror of Man* paints the golden mean between avarice and prodigality (as do all the moralists), and warns the knight against the quest of that glory which is not glory. Even greed, the love of pillage, and sloth, the love of ease, are no worse enemies than pride or vainglory to true gentleness, which comes not from ancestry but from God alone—hence the humility, the meekness, of "the very perfect gentle knight." Tradition speak-

ing through Chaucer's Parson proclaims
that "the general signs of 'gentilesse'
are the eschewing of vice and ribaldry
and serving of sin and the using of virtue,
courtesy and cleaness—and (magnificent
climax!) to be liberal, that is to say,
large by measure."

Strong is the ideal bond between chivalry and commonalty. The *Chess Book*
prescribes as the sixth function of knights
that they ought to keep the people.
"How should plowmen be safe in the field,
but if the knights made daily watch to keep
them. Let the knights keep the people
in such wise that they may enjoy peace
and gather the costs and expenses of
both." And the protagonist in Langland's great allegory, *Piers Plowman*,
shortly after his entrance, swears by his
patron, St. Peter, to keep faith with the
knight:—

> "I'll toil and sweat right gladly, and
>   sow seed for us both.
> And for thy love will labor my life
>   long verily,
> By covenant that thou keepest both
>   holy church and me
> From wicked men and wasters."

This "covenant" was sometimes disregarded by both estates of Englishmen —by knights who preyed upon the people and by the common folk who were (says Chronicler Froissart) of a fell, perilous, proud and disloyal condition, but now for a long time (adds the distinguished visitor) "they have been at good accord together, for the nobles ask nothing of the people, but what is full reason." Of all the sketches of Chaucer's pilgrims, that of the Plowman is admittedly the least individual, the most conventional. Consequently we are not surprised to find that Chaucer is here very close to the traditions of the *Chess Book*. His Plowman is a true and good workman, "living in peace and charity, loving God with his whole heart and his neighbor as himself and working freely for others and paying his tithes fairly and well." Put by the side of this Caxton's version of de Cessolis:—"The laborer of the earth ought to know his God that formed and made heaven and earth of naught and ought to have loyalty and truth in himself, and despise death for to intend to his labor; and he ought to give thankings to him that made him and also he is bound to pay the tithes of all his things." Here and in the mystery plays, Abel is held up to imitation as one who gave tithes freely of the best that he chose; while, as Creizenach has noted, "it is a commonplace of church literature that Cain was a prototype of stingy peasants who tried to evade the obligation of paying tithes to the priests. The murder of a brother seems a mere bagatelle compared with the failure to pay tithes." Literature is wont to assign three rôles to countrymen and countryside—the delicately pastoral, the decently rural, the despisedly rustic. Only at the close of the Middle Ages did the eclogue, the idyl, come into its own; but early and late medieval poets praised the life of the fields, not only as close to the happy state of Father Adam, but as providing the necessary sustenance of society. John Gower's sovereign dislike of peasants is born of no contempt for clownishness, but of fear for the safety of his own order of gentry. He paints the rebels of the Great Revolt of 1381, as a nobleman of the old régime would have drawn the reds of the Midi—swine, dogs, oxen, asses led by a fire-breathing boar. Even when his world survived the bestial onslaught, he denounces the cultivators of the soil as lazy and grasping—each doing one third the work and demanding twice the pay of yore—and capable of infinite evil. The indignant complaints of the choleric gentleman are amply supported by ordinances and statutes denouncing the arrogance and hostility of laborers, and fixing the prices of carters, plowmen, shepherds and swineherds. The traditional peasant of Chaucer and the *Chess Books* has no place in the story of the medieval man of property.

The culminating feature of Chaucer's sketch of the Merchant is the zeal of this financier in keeping up the semblance of solvency:

"This worthy man ful wel his wit besette
  Ther wiste no wight that he was in dette."

That is, he showed such dexterity in doctoring his accounts that no one knew of his indebtedness. This sly stroke finds full warrant in the pages of the *Chess Book*. The Merchant of de Cessolis like Chaucer's includes among his activities money-changing (by the table that is before him in Caxton's woodcut are signified the changers and they that lend money, and they that buy and sell by the weight are signified by the balances and weights). He is warned above all things against contracting debt:—"To owe, it is a shame, and to owe and not pay is a more shame. It is said in the Proverbs that it is fraud to take that thou wilt not, nor mayst not render and pay again." A merchant who fails to pay his debts is as great an offender as he who does not discharge faithfully commissions or restore trust-money. Yet the offense was common enough. Gower, who scores many of the sharp practices of commerce, likewise holds up to scorn merchants who do not pay their obligations—obviously a traditional fault, which furnishes no clue to the personal identification that some readers of the Prologue have sought. Chaucer's stately merchant has only one weakness but that, alas, is the very one which utterly vitiates the man of commerce, and of which conventional precept specifically warns him to beware—financial unsoundness. Chaucer knows not the name of this typical offender, this goodly outside of falsehood. Why seem to identify one among so many?

The Physician's portrait in the Prologue is a composite of conventional features that had already found their way into widely known writings of the time, notably the *Chess Book*. There is absolutely no warrant for identifying such a bundle of stock qualities with John Gaddesden or with any other contemporary practitioner. Every important trait is typical of the profession, not a single touch of the eccentric or personal! Chaucer's doctor is grounded in astronomy. The physician of de Cessolis knows among other things "the measures of the hours and days and of the course of astronomy." He likewise "knows the cause of every malady," for he remembers what Avicen saith in his *Aphorisms:* "If thou curest the sick man and knowest not the cause, whereof, it ought to be said that thou hast cured him by fortune and hap more than by any cunning." The profitable partnership between physician and apothecary, which is as old as "Ecclesiasticus," is developed at great length by the Chess-writers, though without the satire of Chaucer and Gower. De Cessolis insists that a physician should know his authorities, especially the books of Hippocrates and Galen and Rasis and Avicen. To these Kunrat, the author of the German expansion of the *Chess Book*, adds: "Johannicus" and "Haly" and "Damascien" and "Bernard." The last, Bernardus Gordonius, dead at the time of Kunrat's writing, had been his own physician at Montpellier and had cured him of a grievous malady. Bernard thus becomes a man, not a book (*The Lily of Medicine*), while Chaucer's Gaddesden ("Gatesden") is only a name.

Molière and Le Sage are no keener in their castigation of the physician than the medieval satirists—Rutebeuf, Guiot, Gower. His costly dress, his sordid desire of pelf, his lamentable incompetence are constant challenges to derision. And yet another ground of attack is revealed —or perhaps concealed from the modern reader—in the seemingly simple line of the Prologue, "His studie was but litel on the Bible." So far is Chaucer from availing himself of a merely conventional gird at the traditional skepticism of the tribe of physicians that the true implication of the line is revealed only by a study of contemporary unfaith. No verse in all the Prologue has a more definite connotation. The Doctor's "study was but little on the Bible," not because he is a typical physician of any or every age, but because he is a fourteenth-century Arabist and astrologer.

This opinion is sustained by a score of passages in Ernest Renan's scholarly volume of sixty years ago, *Averroes et l'Averroisme*, (1866), a study of the life and influence of the notable free-thinking Moor of Cordova. His illustrations prove beyond doubt that among certain of the orthodox of Chaucer's century, the great Arabian scholar-physicians and their followers are anathema. At the time of our poet's birth, no less than three famous Italian painters, Orcagna, Traini, Gaddi, under the spell of St. Thomas Aquinas, hail Averroës as Antichrist and degrade him to the depths. A French poet of this very date, the author of *Le Tombel de Chartrose*, loudly laments the wide influence of "the cursed Averroës, who was with all his power the enemy of our faith and who chose the life and death of a beast—for no one now lends his ears to hearing sermons from the Bible." Can we wonder then that our Doctor, who derived the larger part of his authority from Arabians—Averroës and six others, Haly, Serapion, Rasis, Avicen, Damascien and Constantyn—should be open to the reproach of neglecting Holy Writ.

The chief witness of the disregard of the Word by contemporary physicians is the illustrious humanist to whom Chaucer owed much, Francis Petrarch. At his town of Padua, medicine, Arabism, Averroism, astrology and infidelity had become almost synonomous terms

(Renan). In his long-winded "Invective against a certain Physician," he accuses the object of his attack of preferring Averroës to Christ and urges him to begin a contemplation of the person of the Saviour. Again in one of the best of his later letters (*De Rebus Senilibus* V, 3), written about 1366 to Boccaccio, Petrarch gives a breezy account of a visit from another Averroist, doubtless a physician, too: "He was one of those who think they live in vain unless they are constantly snarling at Christ and his divine writings. When I cited some passage or other from the Holy Scriptures he exploded with wrath, and, with his face naturally ugly still further disfigured, he exclaimed: 'You are welcome to your two-penny Church Fathers,' etc." Against the background of orthodox distrust of Arabism and astrology, Chaucer's comment upon his Arabist and astrologer, who inconsistently enough devotes his holiday to a Canterbury pilgrimage, seems not only natural but inevitable: "His studie was but litel on the Bibel."

The typical hostler or taverner of our

Chess Book has much in common with Chaucer's Host of the Tabard Inn, Harry Baily. "Hostlers ought to be well bespoken and courteous of words to them that they receive into their lodging. For fair speech and joyous cheer and debonair ought men to give the hostler a good name. Hosts ought to accompany their guests when they depart and teach them the ways and tell them the perils to the end that they may fairly go on their journey." And here we may note that the Host's swearing, which at its best or worst is as "referential" as that of Bob Acres in Sheridan's *Rivals*, and for which the Landlord is so ready to take up the cudgels against Lollards and parsons, is typical of his profession. If the tavern is the breeding-place of oaths, it is inevitable that the taverner should be an adept in blasphemy. Barclay, in a single line of his *Ship of Fools*, gives ample evidence that the Host's cursing is traditional, "Blasphemers of Christ, hostlers and taverners." By the way, the tradition of the shrewish hostess, which we meet in Chaucer, lives on to the days of the "fearful and wonderful Mrs. Tow-wowse" in Fielding's *Joseph Andrews*.

Medieval symbolism finds its happiest or unhappiest expression in the figure and move of the Queen, the sole representative of her sex on the chessboard. Significant difference between our game and that played in the man's world of the Middle Ages!—our queen can move any number of squares at a time, forward or backward, along and diagonal, row or file; while the medieval lady could advance but one square diagonally. And the clerical commentators put the worst possible construction on that oblique move. Saith the so-called *Innocent Morality*, "The Queen's move is aslant only, because women are so greedy that they will take nothing except by rapine and violence."

The lower orders of humanity must be carefully kept in place and restrained in movement. Hence one feature of the chessboard seems to have disturbed mightily the old undemocratic sense of the social fitness of things. Why should pawns, the footsoldiers or commons, stand in front of their betters? De Cessolis offers as a happy explanation of this seeming topsey-turveydom that "the common people are necessary to the nobles and sustain their lives by ministering to them, and therefore are set before them in the play." But a pawn promoted ("queened," as we say) moves obliquely, which shows "how hard it is for a poor man to deal rightly when he is raised above his proper station."

In closing let us view two representatives of the people, churls to the core. The strife between Chaucer's Miller and Reeve on the Canterbury Road is a traditional quarrel of occupations, a class-feud of long standing. From several medieval tracts on Agriculture we learn that the bailiff, one of the three agents under the lord of the manor, had general oversight of all that went on upon the estate, and saw that the lower officers were faithful and active, the demesne properly tilled, the grain properly garnered, the cattle duly tended, the produce sold in the best market, and accounts faithfully rendered to the auditors. On a Norfolk manor the bailiff received for his services two shillings, doubled at a later time, a robe worth twenty shillings (is this not Chaucer's "cote and hood?") and a dwelling at the cost of the lord (the "woning ful fair upon an heeth"). Chaucer's Reeve is like the bailiff in his duties, dealing directly with his lord, out-witting auditors, ruling by terror under-bailiffs, herds and other servants and winning wealth by his purchases.

The relation between Reeve and Miller is so close that William Langland speaks of the two classes in one breath. In Eng-land the sole right of grinding corn, sometimes of making malt, was vested in the lord, and tolls derived from the privilege formed an important item. The privilege he leased to a tenant and put the mill in order for his use. On the Norfolk manor of Fornceth, in the very county of our Reeve's "Baldeswelle," the miller was, in the thirteenth century, a stipendiary of the lord, receiving a fixed fee, but later farmed the mill as a paying tenant. The Reeve, therefore, came frequently to the mill, not only to supervise the grinding of corn, but to collect rents and to supply or resist demands for repairs and machinery. What large room for altercation! Certainly there was no one better fitted than a reeve to pass judgment against a miller's honesty or to illustrate his rascality with a pointed tale.

But in the give and take between the traditional enemies, Miller and Reeve, it is hardly fair tit for tat. The Reeve has an admirable story against a miller very well found, for it fits, as if made to measure, his "deadly opposite," the stout red, wide-mouthed carl of the General Prologue. Simkin, the butt of the story, like his pilgrim prototype, is a good wrestler, handy with sword and buckler, a heavy drinker and a practiced thief (like all millers of tradition), who wins, as the meed of his pilferings, a sharp conclusion from the Cambridge clerks—with changed name the fable is narrated. But the Miller has no story against a reeve. How then can he deal first blow? Chaucer has, however, up his sleeve a churl's tale against a carpen-

ter, quite too good to be lost, so he turns
to the General Prologue, introduces two
lines making the Reeve a carpenter—
and the battle is on. The story seems to
have suggested the trade, rather than the
trade the story, for there is no traditional
connection between a bailiff and the
carpenter's calling. The obvious parallel
between the Reeve and the Carpenter,
who is the victim of the Miller's Tale,
lies not in their common trade, but in
their foolish old age, their futile jealousy,
and their easy deception by their wives,
the traditional fate of Eld mated to youth.
The Reeve's Tale, so potent in its class-
satire against thievish millers, is also
brimful of baffled jealousy; but the Miller
is far too careless a husband to feel aught
but the conviction and penalty of dis-
honesty. Thus the ridicule of classes
and our later theme, the woman question, are blended, now one element upper-
most, now the other. The mating of
class-satire and the *motif* of capital
vices in other quarrels between the pilgrims will be considered in our discussion
of "Sins and Sinners."

II

SINS AND SINNERS

OUR first lecture, discussing the social orders of the Middle Ages, ended with a quarrel of churls on the Canterbury Road. Our second, devoted to medieval sins and sinners, begins with a quarrel of churchmen. The Friar and the Archdeacon's Summoner, as we met them at the Tabard Inn on the eve of their pilgrimage, were genial and jovial, delighting in drink and song, good fellows as Chaucer's venal rascals usually are. But on the highroad near Sittingbourne they are brimful of anger. The Friar, once as playful as a puppy, now "casts the heaviest of scowls upon the Summoner," and the Summoner, he of "the fyrreed cherubinnes face," "quakes for ire like an aspen leaf" and curses and beshrews the Friar, consigning all his kind to hell. Theirs is a conflict not of men but of professions—the long-existent strife between possessioners, the vested interests of the church, represented here by the choleric mouthpiece of the Archdeacon, and the mendicant Friars, who professed to live entirely upon alms. And moreover each tells a story to the discredit of the other's occupation. As in the allegory of *Piers Plowman* (B. V, 136f) this typical contest between the beneficed clergy and friars aptly illustrates Wrath—indeed the rancorous churchmen are Wrath incarnate. And their two stories are examples of anger that knows no bounds. The Friar's tale of a cursing summoner who is carried off by the devil whom he invokes is in full accord with the insistence of Chaucer's Parson in his section on Wrath, that "curses return to plague the inventor." The Summoner's tale is of the fierce anger of a friar, who preaches potently against anger. Now mark the significant irony of the clash between precept and practice—between tellers and their tales. Our Friar's exposure of the cursing phase of Ire is deliciously inapt on the lips of a rancorous man. And his enemy's contribution offers double irony:—in the setting a raging Summoner telling a story against Wrath; in the tale itself a frenzied friar running ridiculously counter to all his own counsels against anger.

The literary implications of this conflict of traditionally unfriendly callings and the closely interwoven moral are three in number. Let us note, first, that in many diverse ways the several classes of society and the chief vices of men meet and mingle in the Middle Ages. Not peculiar to that period is the association of personal representatives of each. In every age the formal portrayal of contemporary "characters" seems to lead inevitably to the juxtaposition of ethical types and social orders. The "Characterisms of Vice and Virtue," so popular among seventeenth-century readers, are soon broadened to include not merely the embodiments of moral excellences and defects, but all classes of men from prince to peasant. In Sir Thomas Overbury's "witty descriptions of the properties of sundry persons," Lawyer, Yeoman, Tailor, Soldier, Sailor divide attention with the Proud Man, the Covetous, the Hypocrite.

As with characters, so with humors.
Ben Jonson's Epicure Mammon, a notable blending of gluttony and avarice,
rubs elbows with Alchemist, Tobacco-
nist, Lawyer's Clerk. Now let us range
backwards to the Middle Ages. In Dances
of Death, Nun, Friar and Merchant are
found side by side with Miser and Glutton. The Morality Plays couple with
especial unction the personified abstrac-
tion and the specialized type. In Lindsay's *Satire of the Three Estates* Chastity is rejected by Abbot and Parson, but
is welcomed by Cobbler and Tailor,
Flattery takes a Friar's form, Falsehood
and Deceit are "leiders of the Merchants
and sillie craftsmen." Sometimes class-
type and sin are mated in one personality
as when Langland pictures Wrath as a
sometime Friar, Avarice as a Merchant's
Prentice at Wy and Winchester, and Sloth
as a Priest and Parson for thirty winters.
More often the alliance between morality and class-satire dispenses with imagery.
The various medieval invectives against
society—the so-called *Bibles*, *Mirrors*,
Estates of the World—denounce the spe-

cial evils of every calling:—the world-
liness of prelates, the laziness of monks,
the avarice and false-witness of lawyers,
the fraud of merchants. Each one of the
various degrees of society has departed
from its true virtue and the deadly
vices have rule over the whole.

Secondly, let us remember that the
literary *motif* of "clash between precept
and practice" is in no way Chaucer's
monopoly. The painter of vice, heavily
tarred with his own stick, has always
been the butt of the satirist. In Juvenal's
Second Satire it is the moralist who is
most corrupt: the creature, "surfeit-
gorged and reeking from the stews,"
chooses abstinence for his theme; the rebel
complains of sedition, the robber affects
to hate a thief, the redhanded denounces
murder, the incestuous emperor restores
the bitterest laws against the sins of the
flesh. False Seeming in the great medieval allegory, *The Romance of the Rose*,
doubly anticipates Chaucer's Pardoner
by preaching against abstinence, though
he loves good dishes and bright wines,
and by exalting poverty, though his bags

overflow with coin. In Dean Swift's *Beasts' Confession* brutes and men are redolent of the faults that they condemn most loudly. All this is not merely the irony of the humorist, it is simple truth to life. Your drunkard hiccoughs potent imprecations against a drunken world. Your craven is quickest with taunts of cowardice. He who wears the scarlet letter upon his heart reveals to others the yawning depths of their guilt. What adviser recks his own rede? The Canterbury pilgrims show, like Ophelia's ungracious pastors, "the steep and thorny road to heaven" and tread themselves "the primrose path of dalliance." Of their inconsistencies, more anon!

Thirdly Chaucer's illustration of Wrath in the quarrel of Friar and Summoner and in the unconscious irony of their tales naturally suggests the place of that vice or passion among the Seven Deadly Sins, duly inventoried and subdivided in the Parson's sermon, which "knits up and makes an end" of the Canterbury stories. Such a classification is doubly in accord with medieval taste and tradition. Scholasticism ever encouraged the framing of formal categories, the schematic grouping of topics, the methodical reduction of all things to a definite system. The conditions of men, their studies whether of philosophy, art or science, their faculties, habits, actions, virtues and vices must be linked in due succession. "Order was the first law," not only of heaven and its hierarchies, but of earth as well. Men lived, and loved, served and fought—and even sinned in accord with codes and catalogues as rigid as they were often wrong. The Seven Sins became as firmly fixed in the moral scheme of things as the Seven Sciences in the intellectual sphere and the Seven Planets in the physical universe—but unlike them endured long after the Middle Ages came to an end, and indeed still have power to inspire sound Lenten discourse.

Samuel Butler, he of *The Way of All Flesh*, remarked very wisely: "People divide off vice and virtue as though they were two things, neither of which had with it anything of the other. This is not so.

There is no useful virtue which has not some alloy of vice, and hardly any vice, if any, which carries not with it a little dash of virtue. Virtue and vice are like life or death, or mind and matter, things which cannot exist without being qualified by their opposites. * * * The highest ideal we can conceive will yet admit so much compromise with vice, as shall countenance the poor abuses of the time, if they are not too outrageous." All this might be aimed directly at the typical medieval mind, which sanctioned no homage from virtue to vice, or from vice to virtue. The formalists of that era conceived of the vices as extremes in the Aristotelian sense, with which any compromise was impossible. With them every man was God or Devil. Fortunately the greatest poets of the era, when availing themselves of the convenient formula of the sins, softened its rigidity with large sympathy and understanding. Dante discovers in the chief forms of vice merely perversions of love, poisoned fountains of spiritual energy. And Chaucer is always so humanly aware of the

good in the bad, and of the bad in the good
that he never views men as mere personifications of this or that evil.

For many centuries medieval moralists groped their way towards a classification of the Deadly Sins that should
be final in number, names and arrangement. Apparently there was no direct
inspiration in the leisurely framing of
that fearful sequence. During five hundred years—from 450 to 1000 A. D.—the
number is usually eight, and the names
vary slightly in the lists sanctioned by
different authorities. Yet, if we com-
bine Pride and Vainglory, the sequence
of St. Gregory at the beginning of the
seventh century differs in no way from
the arrangement most popular in the
thirteenth or fourteenth—that of Dante,
Chaucer and Gower. Henceforth, save
for occasional shifts in order, the Deadly
Seven maintain their bad eminence in
all categories:—Pride, Envy, Wrath,
Sloth, Avarice, Gluttony and Lust. Pride
is always the crowning vice—the head
of all offending, queen and mother of
the others; by this sin fell the angels,

for this sin man lost paradise, and the
souls of men suffer through this taint
their deepest corruption. / Indeed the
so-called spiritual vices are placed higher
in the scale of sin than the carnal. The
infernal brood became as familiar as
their father, the Devil, to every layman,
for it was the policy of the medieval
church to expound regularly the com-
mandments, the creed, the virtues and the
deadly sins—no less than four times a
year according to a ruling of the Synod
of Oxford (1282). A knowledge of the
nature of the Seven Vices was the aim
and end of all instruction before confession, then as now an important part of
the sacrament of penance. Hence their frequent appearance in manuals, penitential
songs and sermons, treatises and books of
examples. Their presence is no intrusion,
as some have thought, but an essential element in the discourse of Chaucer's Parson,
with its conventional divisions of Contrition, Confession and Satisfaction.

Let us recall the last and only confession of that outrageous sinner of the first
story of the first day of Boccaccio's

Decameron, Master Chappelletto. Although a slave to every vicious joy, without one saving grace, the monster wins readily absolution from the good friar who comes to his deathbed by the seemingly frank recital of ostensible faults that are but as motes beside the beams of his real enormities. As surfeit-swollen as Falstaff, he declares himself guilty of Gluttony, because, during the Lenten fasts, he had drunk water with too great an appetite; a robber and pillager and caster of cogged dice, he confesses the sin of Avarice, inasmuch as he had done a little trafficking to gain money for God's poor; a terrible blasphemer of God and the saints and the most choleric of men, he freely acknowledges that his Wrath was constantly kindled against young men who curse and forswear themselves, haunting the taverns, visiting not the churches. And so with the other sins! Hence the pretended penitent is not only honored with solemn vigils and a splendid tomb, but, by reason of his posthumous fame, is styled Saint Chappelletto and deemed a worker of miracles.

The doctrine of Seven Capital or Deadly Sins still receives ecclesiastical recognition and sanction; and sermons on these traditional vices, constructed with scrupulous regard to the medieval formula—definition of the sin in question, its branches or subordinate faults with apt examples from human experience, and finally the remedy or opposing virtue—seldom fail of their moral and spiritual appeal to modern congregations, even though men of to-day rarely conceive of sin in separate compartments and categories. As students of literature, we can ill afford to ignore a classification which forms the backbone of the structure of Dante's *Purgatorio*, which provokes the liveliest realism of Langland and the fiercest fantasies of Dunbar, which provides perhaps the most memorable pageant in Spenser's splendid gallery, which kindles ever and anon the subtle irony of Chaucer, which lifts even Gower to the level of visible poetry, which dictates some of the finest passages of medieval prose, which points the moral of a hundred nameless dramatists, satirists and fabulists. The sins are deadly, but, save in an academic lecture, they are seldom dull.

Poetry and the penitential—what in common have these two? The way of penance, under the guidance of Chaucer's Parson, seems a prosaic journey along the weary levels of theological commonplaces. The same road, with Dante as our companion, ascends the triple stairs, the zigzag passes, the girding ledges of the Purgatorio to the Terrestrial Paradise,—at every stage mingled pleasure and pain, the joys of hope, the pangs of purification; at each upward step, fleeting visions that cleanse the mounting soul of passion-stains. Everywhere in the transformation of old conventions and categories perfect beauty and completeness—infinite variety in the parts, absolute symmetry in the whole. The Gate of Purgatory is the tribunal of Penance—its three steps are Confession, Contrition, and Love or inward Satisfaction. And the Seven Sins, whose ledges or terraces we scale, are linked by their inverse relation to the sovereign law of love. Love, the source or principle of all action, is good when directed towards God and virtue, bad whenever misdirected. Love of evil things appears in Pride, Envy and Wrath; too weak a love of good things in spiritual negligence or Sloth; too strong a love of things, that are good in moderation, Avarice, Gluttony, Lust. Such logic we may match in Aristotle or Aquinas. Art enters in rich measure in the penalties of the sinners:—the proud creeping under heavy masses of stone; the envious in livid haircloth, with baleful eyes sewn up; the wrathful befogged with blinding smoke; the slothful speeding in zealous haste; the avaricious bound hand and foot and prostrate in the dust; the gluttonous tortured by the curse of Tantalus; the lecherous purified in a fiery furnace. In each of the seven circles is not only a proper form of punishment, but a proper theme for meditation— examples alternately sacred and profane of the vice, succeeding those of the corresponding virtue. And at the end of the stay on each terrace, while blessed voices

chant an apt beatitude, an angel of
the antitype, Humility or Charity or
Peace or Diligence or Chastity, wipes
away from the poet's brow the stigma
of the sin. How impressive the plan,
and how harmonious the execution!

Medieval delight in subdivision and
specification assigns to each of the Seven
Deadly Sins a bestial brood of evils.
Church Constitutions directed every
parish priest to instruct the people not
only in the Capital Vices, but in their
progeny as well. And in dozens of monstrous family trees now unhappily ex-
tant, the ramification extends not merely
to branches but even to petty offshoots
and twigs, so that each peccadillo can
display its quarterings. The image of
parent vices and daughters that we meet
in St. Thomas Aquinas is preserved in
Gower's *Mirror of Man*, where each
principal vice is the daughter of Sin and
Death, and each in turn, by union with the
World, begets feminine offspring. But
perverted fancy is not content with this
human figure. The smaller faults are
sometimes boughs from tainted trunks,

sometimes oozes of filthy bogs, sometimes whelps of vile beasts. These strange categories often vary widely in details, but their likenesses are quite as striking as their differences. We may reasonably expect to find, as in Chaucer's Parson's Tale, Hypocrisy, Vainglory and Disobedience as subheads of Pride, Detraction and Grudging of Envy, Hate, Chiding and Homicide of Wrath, and so with other natural or unnatural derivatives. All this would seem to promise only tedium— and we yawn in fearful anticipation.

Now see what literature has done with this unpromising material. Superlatives are notoriously dangerous; yet I venture to say that the finest passage in all English prose during the three centuries between the end of the Anglo-Saxon period and the days of Richard Rolle and John Wycliffe is that portion of the *Ancren Riwle* or *Rule of Nuns*, which deals with the Sins and their progeny. Scholars have recently been at odds over the date of this admirable treatise penned by some good old churchman for the guidance of recluses; but no one has remarked that the elaborate development of the Sins motive assigns the original composition of this fourth section of the book to the period after 1200. The preacher warns his dear sisters, the gentle anchoresses, that evil beasts are lurking in the wilderness on the way to the blessed land of Jerusalem—the lion of Pride, the serpent of venomous Envy, the unicorn of Wrath, the bear of dead Sloth, the fox of Covetousness, the swine of Greediness, the scorpion of foul Lechery—these and their many dreadful whelps. The symbolism is largely traditional, and the bestial genealogy is painfully familiar. But the mentor indulges his own copious fancy, and his unerring instinct for the right word—rare gifts in that day and hour—in his lively pictures of the chief officers in the devil's retinue. "The proud are his trumpeters, drawing in the wind of worldly praise and then, with vainglory, puffing it out again; the envious are his jesters, twisting their faces, distorting their mouths, scowling with their eyes. The wrathful man fences before the devil and juggles with the blades of cutting words; the slothful sleeps in the bosom of the fiend and lovingly receives his lessons; the covetous is the ash-gatherer of Satan, raking together and heaping high his piles of dust; the greedy glutton is the devil's own manciple or purveyor, haunting cellar or kitchen, his heart in the dishes, his life in the tun, his soul in the pitcher; and lastly the lecher, in the devil's court, defiles himself and all his fellows." The sure progress of each of these sinners to his infernal punishment is traced with the flagrant art that makes the most of vivid detail and of lurid climax. Wonderful work for that stage of our prose!

The poetry of England realizes the highest possibilities of our familiar theme. Nothing in all Langland's great allegory of *Piers Plowman* pierces more invectively to the heart of those evils that assail contemporary life than his Shrift of the Deadly Sins; nothing in Dunbar's varied verse compares in mastery of the swift, the glowing, the grotesque with the Dance of the Seven Deadly; and certainly nothing in John Gower's Latin, French and English equals in stately impressiveness the pageantry of his mounted Procession of the Sins—a medieval tradition that flowered magnificently two centuries later in the first book of *The Faërie Queene.*

William Langland, whom I cannot believe to be, like Mrs. Malaprop's "Cerberus, three gentlemen at once," makes each of the penitent vices an intensely personal power for evil in the everyday world about him. Pride is a woman, Pernel Proudheart, who is punished by a hair-shirt, for, as we shall see in our next lecture, the love of rich raiment is one of the several medieval reasons for linking women with the chief of the sins. Of Lechery we learn nothing worse than that he is a sabbath-drinker, who henceforth will drink but with the duck. Envy is drawn at full length— always pale, lean-cheeked, scowling and striking with words that sting like adders' tongues—a bad neighbor, who, like Holy Willie, breathes at the very altar curses against those about him and backbites them in shop and street. White-eyed, sniveling Wrath is a friar, who, like Chaucer's, is always at odds with the possessioners or vested interests of the church; but he has served also as cook in a convent kitchen and stirred the nuns to jangling and chiding. Avarice, beetle-browed and wrinkled, has been a merchant's apprentice at Wy and Winchester Fairs, and has mastered all the small tricks of tradesmen and money-lenders. Gluttony stumbles into a tavern of the time, as real as any alehouse on Thames Street or East Cheap, and among boon companions of the lowest stripe sings and swears and swills until the inevitable collapse, followed by the morning-head. And Sloth, slimy and beslobbered, is a parson, illiterate and negligent, knowing old balladry better than his pater-noster, and missing matins and mass when any distraction—like the Reverend Laurence Sterne's Sunday covey of partridges—calls him afield. Every line of Langland's "rom, ram, ruf" impales some fault or failure of commonplace fourteenth-century humanity. And the shriving of these shrews or scoundrels carries small hope of thorough godly reformation.

The headlong verse of William Dunbar's *Dance of the Deadly Sins*—writ in broad Scots a century or more after Langland—sweeps us far more swiftly than Tam o' Shanter's Meg bore her drowsy master away from town and tavern to a veritable witches' Sabbath of hideous revelry. Even Burns' dreadful warlocks of "Alloway's auld haunted kirk" can scarcely vie with this fleeting vision of "the wildest grotesquerie wrought on a background of penal flame" (so Alexander Smith in *Dreamthorp*). On the night of Shrove-Tuesday, carnival time (February 15, 1507), the Devil among his friends wills that "shrews that never were shriven" shall dance before him in the fashion of France. And the Deadly Seven begin to leap at once, Pride in the van, hair thrown back and bonnet on side, with all his train, skipping through the fire. Then, "with sturt and strife," Ire, knife in hand, leads an armed throng of boasters and braggarts, who strike and stab with sharp swords. Next trembling Envy, filled with feud and felony, is followed by backbiters and

flatterers and calumniators and "all the
human serpentry that lurk in the courts
of kings." The Avarice stanza is one
of the most vivid:—

"Next him in dance came Covetice,
 Root of all ill, and ground of vice,
  That never could be content.
 Caitiffs, wretches and usurers,
 Misers, hoarders, gatherers,
  All with that warlock went:
Out of their throats they shot on other
Hot molten gold, methocht, a fother (*load*)
  As fire-flaught maist fervent (*lightning*)
Aye, as they emptied them of shot,
Fiends filled them new up to the throat
  With gold of all kind prent." (*every coinage*)

With them, too, danced Sloth, like a sow
out of the midden, and his sleepy crew,
lashed on the loins by Belial's bridle
reins; foul Lechery and his band, whose
evil faces gleam like burning torches;
and, last of all, unwieldly Gluttony and
the drunkards of huge paunch "with can
and collop, cup and quart," to whose
gaping lips the fiends gave hot lead to
lap. So the strange shapes pass to the
music of Hell's solitary minstrel, a glee-
man that had killed his man. The fierce-
ness of the imagery frightened somewhat

that good pseudo-classicist, Thomas Campbell, who feels that "it would be absurd to compare this with the beauty and refinement of the celebrated 'Ode on the Passions' by Collins." Lowell, who has little sympathy with the early Scotch poets, deems the *Dance* wanting in everything but coarseness. What would these critics have? Do they seek the graces in Hell's pit? The suddenness and weirdness of the flaming pictures, the boisterous energy of the highly alliterative verse, the humorous expression of serious conceptions, the force and freshness of the forms that clothe familiar traditions, render the poem wonderfully dynamic—yet another signal triumph of the old motive!

The Procession of the Sins has been as provocative of great poetry as either Shrift or Dance. In the fourth canto of the first book of Spenser's *Faërie Queene*, Pride drives forth from her stately palace (the House of Pride is an old motive) in a golden chariot drawn by six unequal beasts on which ride her six sage counselors:—Idleness in monk's garb upon

an ass, Gluttony upon a swine, Lechery
upon a goat, Avarice upon a camel,
Envy upon a wolf, Wrath upon a lion.
Each sin bears in his hand an emblem
of the vice, and each suffers from a
dread disease. In John Gower's *Mirour
de L'Omme* (*Mirror of Man*), a long
Anglo-French poem of two centuries
before, the Seven Sins ride to their
marriage with the World,—whose false
heart seems great enough to include
them all—on animals whose nature is
akin to theirs. A direct connection
between the two passages has been suggested, but Gower's *Mirour*, which was
never printed and which disappeared for
many centuries, until its recovery a generation since, was probably inaccessible
to Spenser—and, even if within his reach,
unreadable. Moreover there are such
notable differences in animals, emblems
and diseases between the two sketches
of the Sins, that I am inclined to regard
the poets as linked only through their
common use of a very variable tradition.
We encounter this tradition of mounted
sins not only in the fifteenth century

poem, *The Assembly of the Gods*, but, interestingly enough, in the three surviving illustrations of the Parson's Sermon in the Cambridge manuscript of *The Canterbury Tales*—Envy on a wolf, Lechery on a goat and Gluttony on a bear. Possibly such mounted figures were frequent on the canvas, tapestry and glass of the late Middle Ages. The medieval pageantry makes a swan-like end, fading in Spenser's music.

Much in the medieval drama is born of the allegorical temper which is always eager to translate spiritual truths into bodily equivalents. And though the constant—indeed conventional—incarnation of isolated moral qualities would seem at first sight too unconvincing a process to awake in any lover of plays a sense of life and reality, yet large appreciation has never been lacking. The morality of *Everyman*, true product of the old materializing habit of mind, captured twentieth-century audiences whether in an Oxford quadrangle or in a Broadway theater. Even dearer to the medieval spectator than this "summons of Death" was the dramatic version of the conflict between Vices and Virtues. Such a struggle has its literary beginnings in the Homeric clashes of worthy and wicked personifications in the popular *Psychomachia* of Prudentius in the fourth century; and, with the universalizing of the formula of the Seven Deadly Sins and of their antitypes, the Cardinal Virtues, the encounter assumed the inevitable form of the beleaguering in town or castle of the powers of good by the powers of evil. In the later pages of *Piers Plowman* Pride, carrying the banner of Antichrist, leads the Vices against the fortress of Unity or Holy Church, which is gallantly defended by the followers of Conscience; and three hundred years later, when the Seven Deadly themselves had ceased to terrify, new champions of Diabolus beset the subjects of Emmanuel in Bunyan's town of Mansoul. So the Castle of Perseverance, in the play of that name, one of the earliest and finest of all the English moralities, must stand a like siege. Mankind has been led thither by Shrift and intrusted to the

care of the ladies of the castle, the Seven
Virtues, who bravely resist the attack
of the World, the Flesh, and the Devil
and their attendants, the Sins. Single-
combats between the traditional op-
ponents end in the repulse of the Vices,
who are routed by roses, emblems of
Christ's passion. With half a dozen
exceptions all the moral plays are devoted to some phase or other of the
spiritual struggle, but the encounters are
usually of words rather than of weapons.

Sometimes the attack of the Sins is
more personal, as when they assail, at
the bidding of Satan, the soul of Mary
Magdalene, and accomplish her downfall
for the nonce. Losing her in the end,
they are soundly beaten by the Devil for
their carelessness. Sometimes they come
in single spies, rather than in battalions.
In *The Interlude of Youth* Master Pride
attaches himself to Youth as a "servant
of price," and fosters in him such arrogance and presumption that he seems,
in his own eyes, king eternal, above duke
and lord and baron and knight, until he
learns a new way of life and bows his

heart at the shrine of Humility. What a world away from such bloodless abstractions is the throbbing reality of Meredith's Richard Feverel shutting himself behind a veil of disdain, yet learning at the end that failure means "pride imperfectly beaten out of life!" When passions spin the plot, the master-passion is Pride both in Victorian novel and in medieval allegory. Mark its bad eminence in the moral play of the days of the Armada, *Three Lords and Three Ladies of London*, where Pride appears as the first of the Spanish lords. We think of Shakespeare's Spaniards, Don Armado and the Prince of Arragon, so sure of their deservings.

If medieval morality found one artful ally in allegory, it employed another accessory, equally ready to do its bidding, in anecdote. Men of the Middle Ages had a childlike love of story, and were always clamoring for new tales, Romances, chronicles, legends, saints' lives, fables, *fabliaux* and beast epics had always the power to charm. Preachers and teachers soon became aware

that their hearers responded far more
quickly to lessons drawn from the actual
experience of men than to formal precept, and welcomed the amusing yet
edifying incident rather than the subtle
argument. And so there came into vogue
the *exemplum* (or "example"), a short
narrative designed to point a moral or
to pound home a text. As these concrete
illustrations were drawn from all possible sources, volumes of every sort from
oriental apologues to barnyard sketches
of cock and fox were plundered for the
making of numerous example-books. Because such aids to religious instruction,
sometimes with index and cross-refer-
ences, were easily accessible, the discourse of the monkish sermonizer was
often drawn less from the gospel than
from the *Gesta Romanorum* and kindred
collections of moralized tales. Indeed
medieval sermons were often, like our
after-dinner speeches, mere strings of
anecdotes of slight relevancy; hence
Dante's stern rebuke of those who go
forth with jests and buffooneries to preach
and who swell with pride, if they can raise

a laugh. Now it happened that the high-tide of production and popularity of *exempla* came in the thirteenth, fourteenth and fifteenth centuries, when the *motif* of the Deadly Sins was on its wave-crest. Consequently form and theme are soon combined, and each and all of the fateful Seven are provided with a rich repertoire of narratives more or less fitting. Every one of the Vices is written large across the pages of the famous *Gesta*, most notable of collections. Pride is stripped and whipped in the fifty-ninth tale, that of the Emperor Jovinian, whose variant, the romance of Robert of Sicily, is familiar to every schoolboy in Longfellow's version; and all the vicious fellowship suffer like exposure. Avaricious tavern-revelers, greedy for gold to pay their long reckoning, learn that every blind man shall annually receive a hundred shillings by a decree of the King. So they straightway draw lots, blind one of their fellows and lead him to the King's gate. The seneschal asks the blind man what he wants. "A hundred shillings," replies he, "which the law gives to every blind man." "My friend," says the seneschal, "I saw you yesterday in a tavern with both eyes perfect. The law relates only to those who became blind by natural infirmity." Some of Jacobs' stories of Ginger and Sam in *Many Cargoes* are but milder variants of this medieval *exemplum*. Very grim are the penalties of sin in the fifteenth-century *Alphabet of Tales*, a digest of many volumes:—here a lecherous soul is chased after death by the hunter of hell with horrible horn-blasts and huge barking of hounds and is borne away at last behind his saddle—a medieval motive of wide currency. But these are isolated illustrations of the Vices. Through their close connection with the confessional, the Sins receive their fullest exemplification in penitential sermons and manuals; for treatises like the Parson's preachment of Chaucer, unrelieved by story, exact from their readers a severer penance than that entailed by the gravest fault. Most interesting of English books of the class is the *Handlyng Synne* of Robert of Brunne, abound-

ing in stories that will move men to better
things at games and feasts and taverns.
His tales often reveal capital sinners
against an English background: a miser-
parson of Cambridgeshire, exponent of
Avarice, who, on his death bed, stuffed
his mouth full of gold; two dishonest
executors of Kesteven that would not
fulfill a testament; a bondman of Norfolk who reproved a knight for sacrilege
in a churchyard; a slothful squire of
Lindsay, who put off repentance until
too late—these stories of local flavor came
close to the homes and hearts of men.

The aim of such narratives is practical
—to provide priest and penitent with
moral instruction in the guise of story,
to purge men of gross evil by unseemly
instances of their common weaknesses
—in design and fulfillment little or nothing of the appeal of art! Now enters
somewhat doubtfully, Chaucer's contemporary, John Gower, half moralist,
half artist, partly bent on reshaping a
world out of joint, partly intent on re-
vealing the sentiments of courtly love.
Hence the hundred and more stories

of his *Confessio Amantis*—no misnomer
this, for the *Confession* is the lover's
shrift of deadly sins to the priest of Venus
in the systematic fashion of the customary penitential with the stock questions and answers. Extremes often meet
and mate in the Middle Ages, but what
possible bond between the deadliness of
the Vices and the daintiness of amorous
fancies? To justify such a union we shall
range afield in the pleasant company of
a young hero of romance—Petit Jehan
de Saintré. Little Jehan was page to
King John of France in days when Gower
himself was young. The pretty story
runs that the boy wins the notice of a
lively young widow of the court, the Lady
of the Fair Cousins, and is bidden to the
presence of this dame and her woman.
He is duly catechized for their sport,
blushing the while for sheer ignorance of
all the art of fine loving. The lady then
becomes his mentor, and puts him through
the paces of courtly training. And
the very first lesson in the gay science
that thirteen learns from the lips of twenty
is not dexterity in twirling a fan or in

thrumming a lute but salutary doctrine indeed—how he, as a lover, may best shun the Seven Deadly Sins. He will escape the Pride of wit and wealth and beauty if he is ever humble and courteous and gracious in the service of his *amie;* if he is joyous and patient—and the true lover must be both,—he will flee Wrath; and avoid Envy, too, if he is truly noble. Avarice cannot cope with the lovable virtue of largesse, nor Sloth with the duty that he owes at every hour. The abstinence that overcomes Gluttony and the self-mastery that defeats Luxury are necessary to the nature of him who hopes to stand in his lady's grace. As a gallant victor over vices little Jehan is trained—and indeed many a courtly neophyte. So the two conventions, one born of Gregory and the Fathers, the other of Ovid and the Troubadours, blend in life and in letters. Sustained by the tradition of this alliance or mis-alliance—which we meet, by the way, in Chaucer's *Troilus*—Gower combines authority and entertainment in his med-ley of sacred and profane love. As he

weaves with divided purpose his century
of tales—the double identity of the writer
is manifest. He is, as Chaucer called him,
the "moral Gower," the mature homilist
who had already, in his *Mirour*, exor-
cised grimly the devil-born brood of
vices; and he is, in the same breath, the
courtly Gower, the man of sentiment,
sweet chanter of his lady's charms in
ballades of chivalrous devotion. In this
dualism of rôles, this harlequinade of
heavenly and earthly obligations, the poor
poet is pulled hither and yon to the ultimate wrecking of both art and ethics.
The man of morals bows his knee to
Venus, the priest of love champions
celibacy. And when confusion is already confounded, there enters to complete our distraction a third self, the political theorist (of the *Vox Clamantis*),
charged to the brim with supposed
Aristotelian precepts anent the duties of
a king. Lowell's damning depreciation
of Gower, "undertaker of the fair medieval legend, whose style has the hateful
gloss, the seemingly unnatural length,
of a coffin" does him *grave* injustice;

for he is a fluent, lively and pointed
story-teller, moving lightly on the four
feet of his verse. Yet Gower's sculptured
head that rests on his three books, Latin,
French, English, in St. Saviour's Church
at the end of London Bridge, has always
seemed to me a symbol of a mind dis-
traught by the effort to run at once on
the three tracks of class-satire, deadly
sins and courtly love (the themes of
our three lectures). When his story
of inobedience, the metamorphosis of
the loathly lady, when his tale of detraction, the misfortunes of the good
Constance, so oft maligned by Envy's
tongue, and when his morality of the
tale-bearing Crow are placed side by side
with their analogues, Chaucer's narratives of the Wife of Bath, the Man of
Law and the Manciple, easy movement
and picture-making power yield to keen
irony and a sure sense of dramatic and
spiritual values.

The device of transferring to a native
background good stories that aptly point
the desired moral seldom fails to render
readers or hearers attentive and teach-

able; but there are other modes of illustration which are even more effective in
their personal appeal. First among these
is the introduction of figures familiar to
the audience. That this or that sin was
committed in a peculiar way in the next
township or county stimulates interest
less than if the sinner were known to all
men present. So when Dante encounters
in the second circle of Hell his friend
Guido's daughter, Francesca da Rimini,
who, as Carlyle says, "may have sat
upon the poet's knee, a bright, innocent
little child," every ear harkens eagerly
to the rigorous punishment of unlawful
love. Or when, descending into the
circle of the rain-soaked gluttons, he
sees on the ground that huge feeder,
Ciacco the Florentine, fellow-citizens of
the unhappy wretch were moved to
purifying pity. Again when the two
poets, Virgil and Dante, furiously assail
the furious shade of one who is now like
unto swine in mire, but who in life was
that "exasperate spirit" of Florence,
Phillippo Argenti, all Tuscans shuddered
as they read. Thus the dread penalties

of Lechery, Gluttony and Wrath were brought home to men.

We smile grimly when Dante and his guide wrathfully assail the anger of the man of wrath. Such opposition of practice to precept has been the frequent theme of satire, for the Comic Muse, as we have seen, sheds her silvery laughter in rich volume upon those sermonizers who incarnate the very vices that they explicitly condemn. Let us now return to the fellowship of the Canterbury pilgrims, which furnishes several striking instances of the ironical association of sins and social types. With the goal of the journey, the great cathedral, in sight, the Parson "knits up the feast and makes an end" by means of a penitential sermon of the conventional type. This is well adapted to time and place and loved ones altogether, for the hearers, men of many professions, have been tarred more than once along the way by the black brush with which they smear fellow-sinners. And even though scholarship has labored, in despite of one poor interpreter, to acquit these pilgrims of sundry faults, their errors often cry out for the good priest's absolution. In tracking these slips in sensual mire, I shall avoid, as far as I may, the deeper morasses of debatable ground.

May we begin with that precious rascal, the Pardoner, whose theme is always "Avarice is the root of all evil" (*Radix malorum est cupiditas*). But dogma and rule of life are in direct conflict. All his cunning sale of false relics, all his clever discourse against covetousness, are designed to win pence.

> "Thus can I preach against the same vice
> Which that I use, and that is Avarice."

And when the Pardoner is called on for a tale, he selects as an *exemplum* of his favorite text one of the great short-stories of the world, aimed against Avarice in many versions in many lands, and he betters it mightily in the telling. In a town of Flanders, where a company of young folk haunted the taverns, a thousand had been stricken by a great pestilence. Three unregenerate rioters, sitting, ere prime of day, over their drink,

hear the clinking of a bell and learn that
an old comrade has been slain in his cups
by a false traitor, named Death. Pledg-
ing loyalty to one another, they rush
forth in drunken rage with drawn swords
and with curses on their lips to revenge
their friend. On their way to a desolated
village, which may be the habitation
of the enemy, they meet by a stile a
poor old man, "al forwrapped save his
face." He cannot barter his age for
youth, and, though he knocks with his
staff at the gate of his mother earth, she
will not let him in. When shall his bones
be at rest, as Death will not have his
life? "Where then is Death," churlishly
demand the ruffians, and the old man
directs them up a crooked way to a
grove and the shadow of an oak. There
the seekers find not, so it seems, Death,
but the fulness of life—a great hoard of
golden florins. One of the three scoundrels ("shrews") must hasten to the
town for bread and wine, while the
others guard the treasure. In his absence, the two, coveting their fellow's
share of the wealth, plan his murder;

while he, rolling up and down in his heart the beauty of the florins, puts poison in the wine. When he returns, his mates slay him and then drink deep. And thus they all find Death. And the money-loving Pardoner tags the tale with a moral, "Now, good men, beware of the sin of Avarice!"

Nor is our inverted moralist content with one shining mark; but launches the long shafts of his invective at the traditional vices of the tavern, Gluttony and its accessories, Luxury, Hazardry, Blasphemy. This vehement diatribe, which some have deemed a digression, finds fourfold warrant. The rascal's sermonizing is derived directly from the setting of his story. His moralities follow immediately his picture of the Flemish tavern, the abode of drinking, lechery, gambling and great oaths. In this "devil's temple" his young folk play at dice both day and night, and eat and drink to excess; their oaths are great and damnable; and among them is kindled and blown "the fire of lechery that is annexed unto gluttony." The preacher then proceeds

to inveigh against each vice in its turn.
Secondly, the characters of his tale offer
apt illustration of the sins that he has
just denounced. The three tavern rev-
elers or "hazarders," who seek and find
Death, covet gold that they may fulfill
all their desires, and play at dice to their
heart's content; they are deep in drink
("al dronken") and they rend Christ's
blessed body with their grisly oaths. A
tavern, too, is the stage of the Pardoner's
harangues. What infinite zest it adds to
the Pardoner's arraignment of tavern
follies to realize that every count of his
indictment is pronounced amid huge
creature-comfort in the joys of an alehouse—the clink of canakins, the laughter
of tap-wenches, the rattle of dice, the
sound of oaths! The irony of environ-
ment is as delicious as the mockery of
personality—both utterly at variance with
the tenor of the Pardoner's sentences
so gravely delivered. He is selected to
preach against Gluttony and its kindred
sins, as well as Avarice, because a long
tradition brands Pardoners as lovers of
gold and gluttons. A sequel to the

Canterbury Tales, The Merry Adventure of the Pardoner with the Tapster at Canterbury, shows that he was deemed the typical tavern-reveler of the company, fond of both his glass and his lass. In our present context he confesses that he loves liquor of the vine and has a jolly wench in every town; and refuses to tell his story until he has eaten his cake and drunk on the wayside a draught of moist and corny ale. Moreover this professed champion of the Second Commandment is a constant offender against its decree: "by God and Saint John," "by Saint Ronyon," "by God." And thus the Pardoner, gluttonous, lecherous blasphemous, unable ever to resist the lure of ale-stake and petticoat, bibulously preaches sermons against tavern sins from a tavern bench. Moreover what convincing testimony to the Pardoner's repute in the company is given by the cry of the gentles, when the Host heralds this "noble ecclesiaste:" "Nay let him tell us of no ribaldry." The chief tavern-haunter of the fellowship inveighs against the evils of "the devil's temple" in due accord with the irony that makes each sinner denounce his peculiar weakness. The Pardoner unlike other pilgrims ever knows himself. Certainly this arch hypocrite undergoes no "moral convulsion" when he is dilating against Avarice and Gluttony. Through his consummate artistry he hoodwinks his audience. The dexterous juggler can still ply his tricks, even after he had thrown all his cards face-up on the table and revealed his hocus-pocus. In the sight of all the birds, this fowler confidently displays his snare.

At the outset of this discussion we marked the ironical blending by the Comic Muse of professional and moral elements—class-traits and traditional sins—in the quarrel between Chaucer's Friar and Summoner. The same satirical fusion of typical features appears in the encounter of other pilgrims. Our wayfarers had reached the little town of Bob-up-and-down, under the Blee, near Canterbury, when the gross drunkenness of the Cook—the intemperance of whose class was proverbial—calls forth an angry revilement of over twenty lines

of very vehement verse from the Manciple. "And with this speech the Cook
wex wrooth and wraw" (which means
"as wrathful as can be"), and, tumbles
from his horse in drunken rage. The
Host then interposes, and the two pilgrims, through his persuasion, are re-
conciled over a gourd of wine. Then
come the Manciple's story and homily directed with deliciously unconscious irony
against the very fault of which he has
just been guilty—but more of this anon.

The Cook and the Manciple contend
not by chance, but because the one is
Cook and the other a Manciple. The
New English Dictionary's many references
to the Manciple and his vocation show
that from the thirteenth century to the
latest account of the cuisine of an English
college or law-inn, this buyer of victuals
is always associated with cooks and
kitchens. You will remember that in the
"Rule of Nuns" (*Ancren Riwle*) the
glutton is described as "the devil's manciple," for he sticketh ever in the cellar
or in the kitchen." Nothing then could
be more natural than a quarrel between

this overlord of the Temple kitchen and
his underling, a Temple Cook.

But the Cook of London is not a servant at the Temple.   As Chaucer makes
evident, he is the keeper of a cook-shop,
one of the loud-mouthed crew that
cried their pies and pigs and geese at
Westminster Gate or clattered their
pewter pots in East Chepe. The public
cook-shop in London on the river bank
was well-known even in Henry II's time.
The shopman's rascalities were curbed
by strict laws, which he often managed to
evade as is amply shown by Gower's
protest in his *Mirour* against short-
weight loaves, bread-prices boosted by
the storing of grain, lean beef, spoiled
game, vile beef. That our Cook was as
frequent an offender as any, we know from
the Host's words:—

"Now telle on, Roger, loke that it be good
  For many a pastee hastow laten blood,
  (Thy meat pies are old and dry)
  And many a jakke of Dover hastow sold
  That hath been twyes hoot and twyes cold.
  Of many a pilgrim hastow Cristes curs,
  For of thy persly yet they fare the wors,
  That they han eten with thy stubbel-goos;
  For in thy shoppe is many a flye loos."

Surely there was every reason for man-ciples, large buyers of victuals, to quarrel with cooks and cook-shops; that they did so quarrel is demonstrated by Oxford records of the fifteenth century. The victualer, too, had his grievance against his sharp customer, as Chaucer, the vint-ner's son, fully recognized. Of all the pilgrims the Cook has had of course largest experience with the unscrupulous reckon-ings of the buyer of victuals. Chaucer delights in just such fineness of point.

The Manciple's contribution is an admirably human example of the master's ironical method of illustrating the Vices. The Manciple's own chiding tongue riots among the very epithets forbidden a chider of drunkenness by the Parson in his condemnation of Wrath. And yet rebuke of wicked speech is implicit in every line of his tale of Phœbus and the Crow, which had served the same ethi-cal purpose under the chiding phase of Wrath in Gower's *Confessio*. The Crow which has failed to keep its tongue is the theme and warning of the scolding Man-ciple, whose own is unreined. That we may not miss the point, the story is followed by a tremenduous application, the long morality of the Manciple against much-speaking, ill advised. Words that breed contention—whether through scolding or through jangling scandal—are the chider's weapons. And in each kind of chiding the only way is "to keep well thy tongue and keep thy friend." For a scold or chider, fresh from a fray, to assail at portentous length the abuse of speech is of the very essence of irony.

Not the least pathetic of the Canterbury tales is the story of that very virtuous lady, Dame Constance, and of her many sufferings from Envy and false blame. In the *Confessio Amantis* John Gower uses the adversity of this perfect heroine to illustrate the power of Detraction, one of the traditional branches of Envy. Chaucer knew Gower's story and from it borrowed a touch here and there. That he told the tale with the same moral purpose of exposing a deadly sin, is made likely by the little prologue of "grudging" or murmuring against poverty—a fault that the Parson couples with backbiting or detraction. Now this story of false witness is put by Chaucer into the mouth of his Man of Law, the falseness of whose tribe was a by-word. Everywhere in the fourteenth century men of law are hailed as arch-deceivers and detractors. Wycliffe voices a conventional prejudice in his imprecation against lawyers as "special procurators and false knights of the devil to maintain falseness and destroy truth." Others expose the calumny and prevarication of the law-courts and their advocates and denounce men of the profession as basilisks, who poison the air about them turning even honey to gall. Chaucer himself tells us nothing of the Lawyer's guile in an Introduction, which was obviously written for another story than this tale of backbiting. But we must not overlook the irony that puts into the poison-breathing mouth of the professional detractor a story of threefold detraction. The absolute incongruity that critics have remarked between the character of the narrator and that of the narrative thus marks another signal triumph of the Comic Muse, who loves to reveal "men at variance with themselves and their professions."

Two of the Deadly Sins dog the steps of medieval authors—Sloth and Envy. When William Caxton, in his prologue to the first book printed in English, *The Recueil of the Histories of Troy*, announces his intent, through his translation, "to eschew sloth and idleness, which is mother and nourisher of vices," he is but following a tradition rife in the prefaces of many centuries. Far back in Henry II's time, Gerald of Wales is led to the making of more than one book by his desire to avoid idleness. But only Chaucer, I believe, links the prefatory formula directly with the central theme of the work. To escape the trap of Sloth, his Second Nun, representative of the somnolent life of the monastic orders, tells the story of that "ensample of good works," ever active in her devotions, the "busy bee," Saint Cecilia—practice and precept again in conflict!

Everywhere in the middle centuries of our literature livid Envy sits behind the writer as tenaciously as black Care behind the horseman, threatening with gnawing tooth the masters of the craft as ominously as the meanest scribbler that ever dared print. The dread of detraction has other than medieval warrant as the tradition thrives among the classical poets, Ovid, Statius, Martial. But nowhere in literature is this shrinking from criticism so strong as in the Middle Ages. The little book, poem or treatise goes forth in trembling humility, quaking for fear of the venom of envious tongues. This conventional modesty is succeeded in the self-confident sixteenth century by a contempt for the critic, born of the deep-rooted belief current during the Renascence that any imputation of error arises not so much from the weakness of the work as from its envy-producing greatness. Envy always waits upon desert! The modern writer or speaker cannot lay that flattering unction to his soul. Let him, in the present instance, marvel with more than medieval diffidence that his discourse, "barren of eloquence and lame of editing" dare show its face in the presence of men of high repute.

III

THE ETERNAL WOMANLY

A FEW months since, at the General
Convention of the Protestant Episcopal
Church in the United States, an over-
whelming vote of the delegates banished
from the Marriage Service the woman's
promise "to honor and obey" her husband.
And our twentieth century smiles at
the formal passing of a pledge that has
long been regarded lightly. Men of
the Middle Ages were of quite another
mind. Deeming Marriage "a full great
sacrament," they hailed the slightest
breach of the vow of obedience as a crying offense to both God and man. The
first of medieval vices is Pride, among
whose spreading branches is Disobedience
—not only to God and parents, but, as
the old phrase ran, "to husbands and
other benefactors and sovereigns." Wifely
disobedience is deemed so heinous an
offense in the Middle Ages not merely
because it is specifically forbidden by

St. Paul in the fifth chapter of the Epistle to the Ephesians, but chiefly because it holds a dominant place among the deadliest of the Sins. An old Parisian benedict of the fourteenth century, playing mentor to his young bride (we shall meet him later), offsets Petrarch's story of the obedient Griselda with the example of a wife rightly burned for the disobedience into which she was led by her pride —quite as grievous an offense this, so he tells us many times, as the fault of Eve or of Lucifer. Chaucer's contemporaries thus drew no moral distinction between disobedience to God, to king, to master, to father, and the slightest disregard of the husband's wishes:—all are of the deuce damnable. The great Sieur de la Tour-Landry held the same view of wifely duty; as, indeed, three centuries later did Molière's Arnolphe who bids the woman humbly serve her man as "son chef, son seigneur et son maître." And readers of Samuel Butler's *The Way of All Flesh* will remember the genuine distress of Rev. Theobald Pontifex, less than a hundred years ago, when his bride, Christina, shows herself so deficient in duty and spiritual mindedness, "that now upon the very day of her marriage she should fail to see that the very first step in obedience to God lay in obedience to himself." Theobald reasoned in the manner of his medieval predecessors.

But alas, offenders were many. The divine right of husbands suffers sacrilege as often as the divine right of kings. There seems ample reason for Walter Map's eager warning to his old comrade trembling on the brink of marriage, "O friend, a man's highest reproach is a disobedient wife. Beware!" The jealous husband of *The Romance of the Rose* wails loudly because "he wore a fool's cap that day when his willful mate swore obedience in church." And Chaucer's Wife of Bath's creed and conduct are always challenges to due subjection and service. The chief obstacles to universal acceptance of the canon of the husband's sovereignty were two; yet each of them a lion in the way. The first was deemed a mighty power for evil, before which

men cowered with a superstitious fear
of some diabolical thing greater than
themselves. Women, whate'er their
weaknesses, have admittedly this ad-
vantage over men, that, when "they've
settled what they're fain to do, they'll
do it, though the world should rue or
perish. They are creatures of untamable
spirit who will have their way, without
counting the cost." (So Jean de Meung).
To this end the Wife of Bath points the
moral and adorns the tale of the Loathly
Lady whose husband puts himself in her
wise governance. The second enemy
to the conjugal convention of man's
dominance is the system of courtly love
which gave authority to the woman.
From every lover is demanded by the
code of chivalric sentiment perfect obedience to his lady, who in turn is absolved
by love's priests of all obligations to the
third figure in the romantic triangle,
the unhappy lord and master. Hence
any courtly story of "fine loving" (*fin
amour* or *par amour*) may with change of
emphasis serve as a warning or a menace
to husbands. In the famous volume of

The Seven Sages the familiar adventure of the immured dame of the jealous dotard, to whose strong tower love found a way, is narrated to exemplify not, as elsewhere, true romance but wifely untruth. Woman's will and St. Venus in unholy alliance are fatal to sworn obedience.

The "querelle des femmes," the war between the sexes, has been waged since the world began. "In the days of King Rameses this story had paresis." Joseph Bédier, the famous editor of the French *Fabliaux*, points to tales at the expense of women in the patriarchal epoch, to the oldest papyri exhumed from the necropolis of Memphis, which reveal the conjugal misfortunes of Anoupou. Euripides and Aristophanes rejoice in the din of the social battle as in the clashing choruses of the *Lysistrata* recently staged by the Russian Players. Juvenal, writing in "the heroic age of female corruption," sends, in remonstrance to a friend about to be married, his sixth satire, which has not a little in common with the monosyllabic counsel of Punch, "Don't!"

"A young man married is a man that's
marred" becomes the stock quip of jesters of every century. The *Panchatantra*
the Hindoo Pentateuch, now accessible in
Ryder's delicious version, revels in this
theme. But in the Middle Ages the *motif*
assumes a fiercer aspect—"a contemp-
tuous wrath against woman, inspiring
the definite dogma that women are not
only inferior but evil beings, cursed
with all the faults of nature, essentially
perverse, ill-tempered, vain, obstinate,
faithless, thorns in the flesh." "Mulier
est hominis confusio" finds few interpre-
ters so euphemistic as Chaucer, "Woman
is man's joy and all his bliss." The
misogynist is rampant in unmitigated
libels that were popular for centuries:
in *The Golden Book* of Theophrastus
preserved in part by that ardent champion
of celibacy, St. Jerome; in *The Dissuasion from Matrimony* of Walter Map;
in the *Miroir de Mariage* of Eustache
Deschamps; in many of the *Fabliaux*,
those roughly merry tales in verse; and
in several of the narratives of *The Seven
Sages*, notably that most gruesome of

world-famous anecdotes, "the Matron of Ephesus," on with a new love by her husband's bier. Jean de Meung, cynical hater of women, continues, with many a gibe and jeer at feminine frailties, *The Romance of the Rose*, so reverently begun by the devotee of the sex, Guillaume de Lorris. "Bien fol qui s'y fie" ("Mad indeed is the man who trusts her") is the text of a hundred satires. A formidable anthology of famous phillippics against marriage was treasured by that most exasperating of husbands, the Wife of Bath's fifthly and lastly, the jolly clerk Jankin, whose long and unseasonable readings therefrom drove his high-tempered dame to frenzy. The fabulous cow, Chichevache, which feeds entirely upon patient wives, has always, on account of scarcity of diet, a lean and hungry look, while its companion, Bicorne, choosing far more wisely patient husbands as its food, is always fat and in good case. The great Knight of La Tour-Landry, a race of Anjou so exalted that it boasted the possession of a family romance, as a noble Irish house vaunts its banshee, writing in 1371 a book of counsel for his three daughters, fills many of his paternal pages with examples of women who were false or foolish or too free of tongue. Even chivalry that bows its heart at the shrine of beauty recks as little of married wit and wisdom as of a wife's eager wishes—indeed to the knight a woman's will seems willfulness. The Virgin, it is true, often exposes the wiles of Venus, but Mariolatry itself is reared upon an abiding sense of woman's imperfections, a firm belief, so says Henry Adams in his *St. Michel and Chartres*, that "Our Lady, in her essence, illogical, unreasonable, capricious, sweetly feminine, caring not a whit for conventional morality, will arbitrarily intercede in behalf of her sinners with a Trinity that administered justice alone." Deeprooted in medieval tradition is the theme of the recent dramatic spectacle "The Miracle," the substitution of the Holy Mother for the erring nun. Such are the chief expositions of the woman-question as the Middle Ages understood or misunderstood it!

Walter Map's *Dissuasion of Ruffinus from Matrimony* chimes in every chord with the medieval tone and temper. It was a best seller in its own twelfth century; for its lively author boasts that it was "eagerly seized, carefully copied, read with huge enjoyment." At the height of contemporary popularity he incorporates it into his *Courtiers' Trifles*. Later ages, denying the tract to Map himself, and stamping it with the seal of a spurious antiquity, reproduced it in many manuscripts and glossed it with many commentaries. The seasonable pamphlet strives to snatch from unhappy fate a dear friend whom Map finds greatly altered in clothes and carriage, pallid of face, peevish of speech and shorn of his wit, sick with love's malady. In his friend's service Map becomes as trenchantly vindictive as, shall we say, John Knox in *The First Blast of the Trumpet against the Monstrous Regiment of Women:* "May omnipotent God grant thee power not to be deceived by the omnipotent female. Women journey by widely different ways, but by whatever windings they may wander, and through however many trackless regions they may travel, there is only one outlet, one goal of all their trails, one crown and common ground of all their differences—wickedness." Our misogynist then lifts from Cicero an anecdote, which soon became vastly popular: "Pacuvius (the tragic poet) said to his neighbor, Arrius (Attius): 'My friend, I have in my garden a barren tree on which my first wife hanged herself and then my second, and just now my third.' Arrius answered him: 'I marvel that thou hast found cause for tears in such a run of good luck,' and again, 'My friend, give me of that tree some branches to plant.'" Jean de Meung, in the wake of Juvenal, marvels at the choice of marriage, when a stout halter or an open well or a dizzy height insures a swift exit from life. And that dolorous wight of the late thirteenth century, Mahieu, who was forced into wedlock with a college-widow of his university days in Paris, raises loud lamentations to heaven, daring even to tax deity with conduct so difficult to justify as the creation of woman. Thus the antifeministic railers!

There are many other counts in the medieval indictment of womanhood besides that willful love of sway which breeds the sin of disobedience. It becomes a commonplace that she cannot keep counsel, for she will not curb her tongue. "Man was made of earth, woman of bone, the sparerib. Shake a bag of dust and it makes no sound; shake a bag of bones and rattle, rattle, rattle is all you hear!" A man will lose all peace, if, by false tears and treacherous smiles and Judas kisses, his wife wheedles a secret from him. Remember Samson. Among the supposed precepts of King Alfred, wisest of Englishmen, was the warning to those who in their cups wildly babble their secrets to wives, that they will be betrayed to their foes, for "word-mad is woman." There are many variants of the story of the wily husband, Cato or another, who confides to his helpmate an absurd fiction of a murder, and by her indiscretion is brought to the foot of the gallows. If women cannot keep counsel, still less can they be trusted to give it. Solomon taught that their rede is evil and leads swiftly to sorrow. And Chaucer's Cock can plead high authority for his pronouncement:—

"Wommennes counseils been ful ofte colde,
Wommannes counseil broghte us first to wo
And made Adam fro paradys to go,
Ther-as he was ful mery, and wel at ese."

Pride is wedded to dames and damsels. Books of satire and of morality teem with examples of proud women. "A ram's horn will be straight when women leave pride and betake them to meekness." And vainglory is ever rampant in rich apparel—in fair deckings, frills and furbelows and ruffs, in mantles trimmed with marten fur, in cinctures bedecked with pearls, in ornaments of rubies and sapphires, in gaudy shoon and hose. The jealous husband in *The Romance of the Rose* maddens his wife by threatening to clothe her in woolen kirtle, a gown of hempen woof and his own old gaiter leggings. Preachers remind their feminine hearers that the holy women that were saints gave away their best apparel, and, in the next breath, these inconsistent sermonizers mourn that vain ladies always don their gayest robes for strangers and the feats of men, and seldom for God and the feats of the church. In punishment of the pride and disguising of themselves that was among women, Noah's flood destroyed the world. William Langland, in his vivid allegory of *Piers Plowman*, personifies Pride by a woman, with particular reference to extravagance in dress, forbidden by English statutes of his day,—restrictions neither more nor less ridiculous than our own sumptuary laws will seem to an age of greater enlightenment. Strikingly enough, the outward and visible sign of feminine pride of heart is sometimes the long train or more often the lofty headgear long popular—for instance the Wife of Bath's kerchief that weighed ten pounds, the prototype of "the lovely hat." The Knight de la Tour Landry complains that women wear horns like snails and unicorns, and reminds his daughters that the devil sits upon such heads and maketh them bow down for fear of holy water. Chaucer's follower, Lydgate, echoes the cry of a dozen satirists:—"List not of pride, then horns cast away."

Love of pleasure and love of praise, lead women forth to feast and jousts, to processions, preachings and pilgrimages, to plays of miracles and to marriages—the better for to see and to be seen. All their heart is set on the world's toys, although their husbands are not best paid with their outgoing. The worldly duenna, who knew of love the old dance, bids ladies betake themselves to all places where Venus and Cupid celebrate high mass, so that men may press around them to behold their loveliness. "Avoid," cries the careful father, "pert and forward speech and much gossip, for that way lies shame. When all begin to sing and dance, look that ye have a friend or cousin or some servant by you for fear of peril and evil tongues." Wise husbands will do well to busy their wives with house and home, with stock and store and domestic stuff, watching all from day to day.

The *Poetic Edda* (of Scandinavia) had early urged men to trust not the words that women speak, for their hearts were fashioned on a whirling wheel. "To love them," says the Northern singer (*Hovamol*), "is like starting over ice with an unshod steed, two-years-old, restive and untamed—or steering a rudderless ship in a storm or hunting reindeer on slippery rocks." The Middle Ages built up a whole literature of bourgeois jest and of courtly love on the power of women to deceive their lords. Their hearts accord full seldom with their tongues. They are as unstable as a flame blown about by the wind. In their mutable natures is neither trust nor sureness. Mere man cannot cope with them, for they have deceived all the sages, Solomon, Hippocrates and even Aristotle, "master of those who know." Merlin, the old enchanter, succumbs to the wiles of Vivien. Look at Walter Map's women. There is not one among all the ladies of his stories, queens and countesses and wives of common men, that does not entail misery by her mendacity. Henno

cum Dentibus, so-called from the size
of his teeth (rather dental than mental,
said Strachey in reviewing our translation of Map), finds the loveliest of girls
in a leafy grove by the Norman coast
at the noon hour, listens to her pitiful
story, leads her to his home and makes
her his wife. But she proves a creature
like the demon-lady in Christabel. She
turns into a dragon, and, tearing her new
mantle into bits, passes through the roof
with a fearsome shriek, after being
sprinkled with holy water. From one
judge of all. Let men avoid the treacherous nets of designing women! De-
mon-woman or woman-demon, there is
little to choose between them. In the
next century romance tells the same
story of a wholly imaginary Cassidorien,
mother of Richard Cœur de Lion—
as much like his subtle parent, Eleanor
of Aquitaine, as this sort of literature is
like real life.

Yet there were many sensible persons
even in the heyday of medieval conventions who were troubled by a doubt of
the truth and good taste of the long cur-

rent calumnies. Men continued to repeat
them with wearisome iteration, but often
with vehement disclaimers of any personal responsibility for the stock charges.

"Thise been the cokkes wordes and not myne,
  I can noon harm of no woman divyne,"

says the Nun's Priest of Chaucer. Lydgate, in his *Troy Book*, reproduces all
the slanders of his author, Guido, but
hastily adds a postscript in defense of
the sex that had furnished so many saints
and martyrs. Petrarch and Boccaccio
make rich amends for their own vehement diatribes against the sex by such
panegyrics as *The Virtues of Women*
and *Ladies of Great Renown*. And even
Jean de Meung, arch enemy of womanhood, forgetting that he who excuses
accuses himself, prays the ladies to for-
give him for citing the words of men who
wrote before he was born. If these
words are false and unmeet, the ancient
sages from whom he gathered them should
be blamed and not he. Here is a palpable
confession that the chief slanders against
women are derived from the reading of
books, rather than from the scanning of

life, are in short figments of tradition, not fragments of reality. But Jean's apology avails him little with the staunchest champion of dames that those ages knew. The weapons of defense opposed to the darts of men's malice are not those of chivalric homage and courtly phrase, but of sound reason and pointed speech. Christine de Pisan, Italian born and French bred, widowed at twenty-five, battling valiantly with flowing pen for the very existence of her three children and herself in that man-managed world of the late fourteenth century—feminist to her finger tips—offers to lying masculine tongues the reproof valiant. "Great talkers prate great nonsense," Christine stoutly affirms in her *Epistle to the God of Love*. Are all women inconstant and deceitful, because this one or that one has erred? Every man who honors his mother should deem women honorable. Instead men, envious, and jealous, judge women by the worst of their sex. Were not Medea and Dido faithful to false men, she asks to the tune of *The Legend of Good Women*. It was a very poor business on the part of Jean de Meung to devise in his *Romance of the Rose* so many tricks to cozen a poor girl—if so much labor is needed to deceive a woman, surely she is more constant than most clerks say. Women's hearts are naturally charitable, devout and full of gentleness and pity; and their words are in due measure. Obviously, the books that Jean cites were not written by women. And then carrying the war into the enemy's camp, she hits hard by proclaiming, like Shakespeare's Duke in *Twelfth Night*, that men are more "giddy and unfirm, longing and wavering" in their love-fancies. In her Golden Book of Heroines, *The City of Dames*, she denounces those husbands, too common in the age of knighthood, whose heavy-handed brutality renders them as dangerous as the detested Saracens. (For a tragi-comic exposition of the miseries of wives, see Dunbar's *Two Married Women and the Widow*.)

Nor does Christine give one foot of ground in the battle for her sisters thus gallantly begun. She inspires directly or indirectly more than one order or court

of love, the members of which pledge
themselves by vow to defend the honor
of women.   Commonsense thus finds an
ally in chivalry.   The romantic Marshal Boucicaut, the voluminous Chan-
cellor Gerson, even such potentates as
Philip, King of France, and John, Duke
of Burgundy, eagerly assume the leader-
ship of the woman party and the lessening
adherents of Jean de Meung and his
Romance must fight with their backs to the
wall.   The tumult of that vivid encounter
is drowned for the nonce by the roar of a
war of nations—England against France.
Thirty years afterwards the dying Christine, now nearly seventy, pours forth her
swansong in rapturous greeting of a champion of seventeen—the maid of God, the
virgin rare, young Joan of Arc:—

"Mark me this portent! strange beyond all telling!
  How this despoiled kingdom stricken lay,
  And no man raised his hand to guard his dwelling,
  Until a Woman came to show the way.
  Until a Woman (since no man dare try)
  Rallied the land and bade the traitors fly.
  Honor to Womankind! It needs must be
  That God loves Woman, since He fashioned
    thee."
                    (Constance Fletcher's version.)

In this trumpet-blast there is surely a magnificent finality.

The Middle Ages recked little of *chiaroscuro*, the artistic handling of light and shade, but ran inevitably to extremes of expression. Black or white, no softening and toning! As with color, so with form: a keen sense of values, due feeling for perspective, proportion, balance, a scrupulous regard for the golden mean are rarely dominant in medieval life. Realism and idealism are both victims of the overmuch. Philip is either very drunk or very sober. Hence women suffered as much from their friends as from their enemies. Humor degraded, romance exalted—and in the end one perversion of truth seems well nigh as bad as the other. Here are the *fabliaux*, verse-tales of contemporary life, teeming with motives familiar in Boccaccio, Chaucer, Molière. They are not designed to instruct, although a medieval father may warn his son to follow bears, dragons and scorpions rather than "la male feme" (the evil woman) of such stories. They are not necessarily rustic or bourgeois,

for they may tell with gusto of amorous
mishaps of great men like Aristotle,
bridled and saddled and ambling on all
fours under the whip of one mischievous
dame, and Hippocrates, hanging high
in a basket between attic and basement
through the wiles of another; and the
genre, before its passing, serves the literary ends of merry-minded gentlemen of
the court.   But, as a rule, the *fabliau*
is middle or even lower class, the delight
of chuckling burghers and boors.   It is
set in a moral vacuum. Its theme is frequently the triangle of the husband, a
jealous and yet credulous dotard, the
lover, a rascally clerk or priest, and the
wife, easy victor by a cunning that tran-
scends the wit of mere man. Circum-
stantial invention of places and persons
and a vivid instinct for homely detail
impart the semblance of truth; yet the
world revealed is not that of life, but of
comedy where all things befall prepos-
terously.   Here is the amusing topsy-
turvydom of the victory of the weak over
the strong, of the distaff over the club.
If in life husbands had been often thus

"bamboozled and bit," masculine readers would have found little humor in these stories. The *fabliaux* are implicit witnesses not of the liberty of the woman, but of the mastery of the man, in their ironical reversal of actuality. Laughter holds both his sides over the farcical situation of the overthrow of the domestic tyrant, who, wishing to make his truant wife the theme of public jest, bars her from his house at night, and then, by a dexterous trick of the woman, is shut out while she slips in. That there is not only humor of plot in the delicious nemesis of the outcome but humor of character in this clever feminine counterfoil of dull and dutiful stay-at-homes, Molière, best of judges, proclaims by his appropriation of both in his play of *George Dandin*. Many years before this, the earliest of old English comedians, John Heywood, had laughingly lifted across the channel like motives from the French farces. And so the Comic Muse, "obliquely malign," gave high approval to imaginary triumphs of women purchased at the cost of all that the respectable wife of reality held dear. In the present hour of woman's economic emancipation that abject submissiveness of the medieval everyday seems to us far more comic than the spirited rebellions of the world of fancy.

Romance breathes an air as rarified and refined as that of the *fabliau* is heavy and gross; but it is quite as far removed from the everyday atmosphere of reality and morality. The code of courtly love demands of each knight devotion to a lady, as a paramount duty. "Have special care to honor thy dame, as thou dost fare thy worldly ways, and if thou hearest calumnies, bid men hold their peace"—so William de Lorris. The *fins amans* or fine lover is formally precise in the inventory of his lady's charms— waves of golden hair (romance rejects the brunette), forehead of a span's breadth, gray eyes, "bent" or arched brows, straight nose, cheeks in which roses and lilies meet—and then a little mouth, with "two lips indifferent red." The neck is a round tower of ivory, body, arms and hands are long. To the catalogue of beauty are appended the qualities of bounty, gaiety, grace and poise—social rather than spiritual virtues. So perfection is drawn, ever after the same ideal pattern. The devotion of the lover is regulated by principles, ingeniously deduced and compiled from the precepts of Ovid and from the inventions of the Troubadour lyrics, under the authority of noble ladies like Eleanor of Aquitaine and Marie de Champagne. All this "fine loving" is a direct challenge to conventional standards of morality, for love and marriage are in constant opposition. The husband, stupid, jealous, tyrannical, plays as sorry a rôle of stern guardian and proves as easy a dupe as in the *fabliaux*. The perfect lover, be he Lancelot, Tristram, or another, leaps lightly over the walls of his married rival,—always with the connivance of the lady, who is not a whit behind her humbler sister of farce-comedy in trickery and in treachery to her lord. Falseness to the husband—if secret—is no offense to decorum, is indeed essential to the courtly game; falseness to the lover is the unpardonable crime against the code. Cressida's untruth to Troilus renders her name a by-word in romance—not because he was, but because he was not her mate. Had they only been wedded, she would have been quite free to welcome the love of another. So unromantic is matrimony that, when the lovers of romance marry, they still cherish the name of *amis*. John of Gaunt, bemourning his dead wife, Blanche, in Chaucer's *Book of the Duchess* defers throughout to courtly conventions by avoiding the words "marriage" and "husband." The medieval poet thus makes wedded love a fit theme for romance, only by employing the formulas of illicit affection. The Victorian laureate, on the other hand, speaks the language of the domestic sanctities even in the wildwood of classical mythology. Tennyson's mountain nymph, Oenone, once beloved of Paris, cries, "Husband," as she leaps upon the funeral pile. The "Lancelot" and "Guinevere" of old romance are exalted as perfect lovers, despite the flagrant wrong to King Arthur. It is modern morality which tells us in the *Idylls of the King* that Lancelot's "honor rooted in dishonor stood."

And yet men of the Middle Ages knew as well as we that these conventions of courtly love were in direct conflict with Christian ethics. The very framer of the code, Andreas Capellanus, makes due apology for his ritual; and the greatest of all medieval stories based upon this immoral system, Chaucer's *Troilus and Cressida*, repudiates at its close such "worldly vanity and appetites." The author of the *Confession of a Lover* tears off his mask, quite like Bully Bottom in the play, and bids us observe that he is no lion among ladies but moral old John Gower, the same very decorous graybeard, who elsewhere exalts the dignity of marriage and sternly exposes the folly of Lancelot and Tristram. Dante, though weeping with tenderest compassion for the fate of those ill-starred young lovers, Paolo and Francesca, who had made Lancelot's story theirs, is yet constrained by his rigid regard for the moral law to see them whirled away with other victims of dear desire by the racking winds of

Hell's second circle. Love's code was admittedly wrong according to the laws of both God and man, but in its immorality lay its charm for a society in which "the actual relations of the sexes were rigidly prescribed by the church and by feudal practice, rather than by the sentiments of the individuals" (Comfort). Here, as has always been its wont, literature presented things that looked as if they might happen, but as they seldom did in a world where hearts were not free to follow their natural bent, but were mated, often in early childhood, in marriages of convenience arranged by guardians who profited immensely from their wardships of young heiresses, after the fashion of the "trustworthy" sex in business dealings with women. Hence the lure of the amorous adventure of old romance for women readers of the Middle Ages, whose own lives were punctiliously correct. Medieval fiction was the reverse of documentary, for it reflects not the life and morality, but the waking dreams and wandering fancies of its public. It seemed even to

the most exemplary of dames a "literature of escape" from the monotony of the
daily round of virtues. Observers, like
Barrett Wendell, have often remarked
in France of to-day the abysmal difference between the distracting woman of
fiction, a centrifugal force in the social
orbit, and the devoted woman of fact
biding close to the heart of home. This
paragon is the pride of family and folk,
but story-teller and his circle turn eagerly
to her dangerous opposite, for, as de
Maupassant (cited by Wendell) once said,
l'honnête femme n'a pas de roman ("There's
no romance in the virtuous.") Even
the good Christine de Pisan forsakes the
penning of homely advice to housekeep-
ing women anent the rearing of children,
the control of servants, the conduct of
the kitchen for the composition of a
conventional story of lawless gallantry
—merely a gay gesture!

If the gentle reader found in medieval
literature of love a refuge from the hum-
drum existence of her man-made world,
she did not thereby exchange, like her
protesting sister of the present, the bond-

age of the group for individual freedom, but merely bartered one rigid system for another. Love may be a greater and stronger law than any man can give; in the Middle Ages it was every whit as strict, and certainly no less formal. The courtly code of Andreas Capellanus, with its thirty precepts, is a manual of social behavior quite as exacting as the formulas of any domestic tyrant. The lady of romance must be as scrupulóus in avoiding the appearance of evil as the lady of reality in shunning evil itself. Decorum has as many conventions as modesty. Indeed the courtly dame becomes herself a convention,—a composite of traditionally perfect features and traits,—so painfully catalogued that individuality is refined to the vanishing point. Between all these medieval heroines is as strong a family likeness as between those stiff and starched Stuarts in the picture gallery at Holyrood, who seem all to have been painted by one artist.

The lady of Troubadour lyrics and courtly fictions suffered, in Italy, a sea-change into something rich and strange indeed. In France she was of the world worldly; in Florence and Boulogna she is less of earth than heaven. No longer a challenge to the church and its rites, she is so transfigured and glorified that the religion of beauty blends with the beauty of religion. To love the dame of chivalry was, as young Troilus found, a liberal education in all social arts and graces. To love one of the ladies of the South, the worshipper must possess a nobility of nature, a gentle heart, God-granted in the hour of birth:—

> "And so the heart created by God's breath
> Pure, true and free from guile,
> A woman, like a star, enamoreth—"

Not only is mortal woman lifted to the skies to dwell with angels in deepest Heaven, but she becomes a symbol of the divine intelligence, of guidance to "the happiness of life eternal." The sublimation of Beatrice as a queen of blessedness is far more certain than the identification of her human self with the daughter of the Portinari, Dante's neighbor. Everywhere in the *New Life* the fair and gentle Florentine is dowered with a supernatural influence; and in the *Divine Comedy* she is beatified as the dream-Rachel, vision of the contemplative life in Paradise. Thus medieval mysticism exalts womanhood as the image of heavenly purity and holiness.

In scores of lyrics love of the womanly is scarcely distinguishable from the love of the eternal. The woman is deified, the divine is humanized. Henry Adams, in that wonderful book which lays bare the heart of medieval worship, *St. Michel and Chartres*, shows that the singer Thibaut keeps the tone of courtly love in addressing the Queen of Heaven in lines which might have been addressed to Queen Blanche. In many manuscripts *chansons de notre dame* employ not only the verse-forms and rhymes, but the very words of the *chansons d'amour* in the same volume. John Gower concludes his little volume of fifty amorous balades with an address to the Virgin couched in the phrases of courtly sentiment, for he loves her best of all the ladies whom he serves and awaits a rich reward for his loyalty. On the other hand an ecstatic woman mystic of the Middle Ages, like Mechthild of Magdeburg, yields heart and soul to the Heavenly Bridegroom in rapturous strains of passionate self-surrender. Such a blending of religion and passion imparts the warmth and strength of worldly love to spiritual ideals and in turn the depth and tenderness of reverent devotion to the praise of an earthly object. The *fabliau* vulgarizes, the romance conventionalizes, the lyric idealizes to a pitch of perfection above and beyond humanity. Let us turn from the woman of literature to the woman of life, realized in the light of common day.

The old French book of 1393, which serves our present purpose, is fitly preceded by a picture of a man and a maid seated in converse in a many-latticed room of the Middle Ages. No courtly lovers these by their seeming! Nor does the title of the volume, *Le Ménagier de Paris* ("The Book of a Parisian Householder") stir any lively hopes of gentle romance or of the gay craft. Ten minutes' reading shows that these pages have to do with the life of a late fourteenth-

century home and with the precepts of
a medieval husband. Chivalry, which
exalts only love *par amours*, deserts
even a troubadour when he steps within
his own gates, and sits with covered
head, like the worthy of our frontispiece,
in the presence of his own wife. Were
she another man's, what a different
story! And the husband of our book is
neither troubadour nor knight, but he
cuts the very figure which courtly love
has always disdained and execrated, that
of the wealthy old bourgeois, loving mastery and ever crying checkmate to his
young bride. Here in the flesh we have a
frosty January of perhaps sixty discoursing most solemnly to a fresh flowery
May of fifteen regarding her wifely duties. And these curtain lectures of
winter evening to summer morn are
brimful of interest. Indeed we can hardly
overestimate the value of this single-
hearted and narrow-minded exposition
of the old-fashioned orthodox gospel of
man's sovereignty as an instructive contrast to Chaucer's unpartisan presenta-
tion of many points of view in the numer-

ous Canterbury prologues and tales that
treat the marriage question. It is well
that we should know how a lack-humor,
prosaic pedant of the poet's own years
—for the unknown author was in military
service as early as 1358, just before young
Chaucer went to the wars in France
—reacted in his later time to the same
maxims, texts and *exempla* of the marriage
relation that our mischievous humorist
turned to the purposes of art. This smug
old Philistine, with much kindness in
his heart and no poetry in his soul, provides us with the best possible illustration of the proper, the conventional,
the traditional—what every comfortable
domestic tyrant thought and said in
the days of the Wife of Bath and the
Merchant.

The suzerainty of the fourteenth-century lord of the household over his young
bride suggests the rule of Molière's
Arnolphe over Agnes or, as we have already
noted, of Chaucer's January over May.
But the third person in this triangle of
very real life is no impudent young spark,
no Horace or Damien. The master of

this earlier school of wives, the *Menagier*,
has as his rival a figment of his own fancy,
his youthful lady's second husband. Not
for himself but for this fortunate Jankin
of to-morrow he trains the seemingly
docile mind and will of the novice. And
this incredible altruism of the pompous
old dogmatist is humanized by the oft-
implied hope that the homilizing which
is the larger part of him will not be dis-
credited after those later nuptials. In
that new estate, the lady must give to
her husband's health and person the most
devoted attention, for, should she lose
him too, she will be hard beset to find a
third and will dwell forlorn and wretched.
He is constantly looking at happiness
through the other man's eyes, peering
forward with orbs already a little dim into
those early fifteenth-century days when
this green girl of the middle teens will
become the dutiful matron, submissive
and serviceable, in another house than
his. A situation meet for comedy, but
not without its saving alloy of pathos!

The husband's prologue is full of what
his mastership is pleased to call "piteous

and charitable compassion" upon the tender youth that he is molding into womanhood. The child—she is nothing more—may work among her rose-bushes, tend her violets, make her hats, even dance and sing in her little circle, but she must avoid the feasts and dances of people of great estate (one thinks here of the "festes, revels and daunces" shunned by the virtuous Virginia of the Doctor's Tale). Of higher rank than he, she must never shame her blood. In as ridiculously methodical a manner as Arnolphe telling off his "maximes du mariage," he imparts the matrimonial lesson in the form of three divisions, containing in all nineteen articles! The first and most extensive of these divisions is devoted to "la salvacion de l'âme et la paix du mari"—not only Hosanna in the Highest, but peace on the little domestic plot of the earth and good will to one man! Of the nine articles of this portion of the Covenant to Enforce Peace at home, three are devoted to the service of God and Mary Mother, the fourth to the guarding of virtue as in the stories of Susanna and

Lucrece, the fifth to affection for one's husband (be he I or another) after the pattern of Sarah, Rebecca, and Rachel, the sixth to wifely humility and obedience, as in the examples of Griselda and many others, the seventh to regard for the husband's person, the eighth to the care of his secrets, the ninth and last to the duty of diverting with all deference and tact a husband from his follies and indiscretions, as did the prudent wife of Meliboeus or the gentle Dame Jehanne la Quintine.

The pompous monitor thus enters with a drillmaster's zest upon the systematic correction and chastisement of the youthful unwisdom of his "chère sœur"— that this is the darling phrase of the gay-hearted Aucassins to his "mie," Nicolette, serves only to heighten the pitiful contrast between gray ashes and the red glow of young love's blaze. Unlike Robert Herrick, our Parisian pantaloon takes no delight in the disorder of the erring lace or the careless shoe string. Kerchief and coiffure must be so point device that no distracting curl may stray.

Then as now boys' glances were eager.
On her way townward or churchward,
middle-teens must walk with lowered
lids and eyes on earth, casting no look
at man or woman and never stopping
to laugh or chat with a passing acquaint-
ance. Why not at once, "Get ye to a
nunnery!" for the worthy master's doctrine seems better to befit a religieuse
than a matron? With special unction
he reviews the devotions of the day and
embarks upon a penitential sermon, surely
not of his own making, and very like
indeed the harangue of Chaucer's Parson. Here are the same three time-honored divisions of Penitence—Contrition,
Confession, and Satisfaction—and here
under the second head is the same large
space, some thirty or forty pages,
accorded to the Seven Deadly Sins and
their opposites.

Shall we read no books that are not
tales of love, and have no friends that are
not lovers? What *lese majesté!* The lord
and master solemnly commends to the
perusal of this slip of a girl the Golden
Legend, the Apocalypse, Jerome's *Vitæ*

Patrum and other treasures of his library—many of these doubtless as intolerable to her young ladyship as Jankin's volumes to the Wife of Bath. In the pages of Augustine and Gregory the demure disciple will read that a worthy woman, so loyal to her husband as to have never a thought of another man, may be called a maid. Let her bear always in mind those models of married chastity, enshrined in the marriage service, Sarah and Rebecca. And then there were Leah and Rachel, too! "Without jealousy, contention and envy they left everything for their one husband Jacob! How many women would live so peaceably together now under such circumstances! I think that they would fight one another. O God, what good and holy women these were!" The wife's most rapturous reading must be, of course, the love letters of her lord, received "en grand joie et reverence"—and providing, so we should guess, much the same warm food of fancy as the Lives of the Fathers just recommended. She must answer in kind. The poor little bride must beware of all other men, chiefly of gay young springalds of the court, lavish of their leisure, fond of the dance and of wild living. "And trusteth as in love no man but me!" Birds and beasts of every sort, all named at terrible length, love their masters—even dogs who are beaten and stoned—hence women also should love their husbands. "Therefore I pray you," adds our overripe logician, "to love very dearly my successor"—"vostre mary qui sera." Most weighty conclusion!

The curtain-lecturer is now fussily concerned lest his pupil shall fail in some service of humility and obedience to her second husband. She must discharge all the commands of that potentate whether given in earnest or in sport; she must avoid all things that he forbids; and must never question his mandates, especially in the presence of others. Nor has the woman any right to know her husband's reasons. If he wishes to disclose them, well and good, but he will do so as a courtesy and in private, never as an admission of woman's mastery and sovereignty. Like Chaucer, the old Philistine feels that Marquis Walter perhaps went somewhat too far in testing Griselda's submissiveness. He is inclined to question the wisdom of robbing a loving mother of her two children during many years' space and then of divorcing her from bed and board, all this merely to assay her gentleness. He himself would hardly have done so; but he approves heartily of less severe trials, and he is quick to cite trivial tests of docility that recall Petruchio's handling of his Shrew. Indeed, he feels that such experiments have divine sanction, in that God himself tested one woman by telling her not to take an apple and another by forbidding her to look behind. Through disobedience many women have sacrificed the affection of their lords, failing to profit by the example of other inferior beings, bears and wolves and monkeys, which gladly dance and leap and tumble at their master's behest. Quite as well trained as any of these animals was that young woman of Melun who won a dinner for her husband from the Sieur de Andresel by leaping three times over a stick, whereas the Sieur's lady, a creature of blooded stock, angrily refused the jump. How much better, had she consulted her lord's honor! The husband who does not find at home perfect obedience in the smallest things as above can hardly be blamed if he finds his pleasure elsewhere.

Yet what is sauce for goose is obviously no sauce for gander. Troubled by a dull masculine fear that womanly wiles will somehow outwit him at his own game, old lack-logic inveighs against the sacrilege of those irreverent wives who test in small ways or great the affection of their husbands. There was, for instance, that outrageous young woman—"condemned to everlasting redemption" in the eighth story of *The Seven Sages*—who tried her worthy old spouse by cutting down his little fruit-tree, killing his pet dog, dragging away the cloth from the table at which sat many guests. Such excesses as these are committed by women who seek to have their own way, counter to their husband's will.

If there be some special pleasure of the wife which the husband has not expressly forbidden—such oversights seem to have been very rare—the dutiful domestic subject will write to him, in case of his absence, and ask his commands, instead of following her feminine wishes. Thus the damp heavy foot of the hippopotamus tramples every young joy in its path.

Care of the husband's person includes eager attention to his every craving for comfort. Three things, as Solomon said, drive a worthy man from his home, "a leaking roof, a smoking chimney and a chiding wife" (thus, too, the Wife of Bath's old husband). But many things make him turn eagerly homeward—a good fire, fresh shoes and stockings, ample food and drink, beds warm and white and free from pests, windows closed in those glassless days with waxed cloth or parchment so that no flies can enter. Then the sybarite waxes somewhat bitter. If women would only devote the same care to their husbands that men give to their horses, dogs, asses and other beasts—he deserves to be taken at his word—then home would seem a paradise of repose and husbands would long to see their wives, as holy men, after fasting and penance, yearn to see heavenly faces. All the deeply rooted medieval distrust of woman's ability to keep counsel inspires the warning to guard well the husband's secrets. To curb the tongue is a sovereign virtue, and many perils come from much speech. Let the woman beware to whom and of what she speaks, cherishing above all the confidences of her second husband, concealing his faults and follies but confessing to him all her own sins. Half a dozen stories of superhuman discretion support the argument.

Moreover, a woman should advise her lord as carefully as one plays a piece on the chess board, gently and wisely withdrawing him from his errors. If this good office makes him so angry that his cruel wrath may not be restrained, let there be no complaint to friends and neighbors, but quiet weeping and prayer in the lady's chamber. One recalls Dr.

Holmes's praise of the Pilgrim Mothers for putting up not only with pioneer hardships but with the Pilgrim Fathers as well. Graybeard's reaction to the story of Melibœus and his wife Prudence, the same tale that Chaucer tells on the Canterbury road, is significant. He extols the worthy woman not only because she sagely and subtly taught her husband patience in his sore distress, and, with timely arguments, dissuaded him from his mad intent, but because she achieved her end with such gentle tact and sweet humility as not to discredit her husband's mastery. Through haughty claims of sovereignty no woman can prevail, for there is no married man, however poor or weak, who does not will to lord it in his house. Thus the days of chivalry deferred to women!

A gently bred girl of the fourteenth century questioned her husband's right to rule as little as the modern 'Arriet denies 'Arry's perquisite of heavy-handed persuasion. Adam's sovereignty was a conclusive argument—at any rate the rib seldom demurred. Nor could our green young May have perceived that

January was unconsciously shattering his whole ponderous structure of masculine domination when for just one little moment his old heart sings to this stirring tune: "Pardieu, I verily believe that, when two worthy people are married, all other loves are deemed as nought and forgotten save theirs alone. When they are together, they look long into each other's eyes and touch hands, without speech or other sign. And when they are apart, each thinks of the other and says deep down in the heart, 'When I see my dear one, I shall say *that*, I shall ask *this* favour.' All their chief pleasures, their highest desires, their perfect joys lie in doing each other's will; and, if they really love, they care not a whit for obeissance and for reverence but crave only everyday comradeship." The words are so unwonted that their full meaning is hardly caught by the girl, yet they chime sweetly in her ears. And though she is well aware that the master may soon regret the outburst, and will never again utter such heresies, her heart dares hope that the other man of whom her mentor is always

discoursing, "vostre mary qui sera,"
will often talk like that. And so we leave
her musing not upon the husband of the
present but upon the husband of the
future,—

"Whoe'er *he* be,
  That not impossible *he*,
  That shall command my heart and me:

"Where'er *he* lie,
  Locked up from mortal eye
  In shady leaves of destiny."

Our old bourgeois has abundantly
realized for us one point of view—here
certainly is truth, but truth seen from a
single angle. For the larger reality that
lives as the resultant of many forces,
the conclusion of many arguments, we
must turn to the great artist who speaks
in various tones, yet is content to listen
when men speak through him. Before
Chaucer, this tongue or that had vilified
or deified woman. He, the open-minded,
succeeds in picturing women as God made
them by holding the balance between
the two traditions with his sympathies
on the side of good. For every bad woman,
his books make mention of a hundred

good ones and later he increases his
count: "and ever a thousand good against
one bad." He admits to his pages the
clashing conventions of the age. He plays
wittily the stock-rôle of vehement opponent of matrimony, in the "Envoy to
Bukton." He takes the familiar tone
of a servant of Venus by rebuking the
blasphemous traducer of the goddess in
the "Envoy to Scogan." He translates
the *Romance of the Rose*, notable heresy
against the law of love; yet he is eager to
do penance:

"In making of a glorious Legende
 Of Gode Wommen, maidenes and wyves,
 That weren trewe in lovynge al hir lyves."

His blame of Cressida for deserting
Troilus is tempered by infinite compassion
for the wretched woman in her untruth.
But boundless is his delight in Love's
revelation that Alceste, that sublimated
being, great queen of the *Legend* Prologue, is, in all her transcendent grace and
goodness, no other than his own lady
sovereign, be she Alice Cestre or another.
Thus he mounts the heights and sounds
the depths.

The Canterbury pilgrimage is along that broad highway of free speech, where every man reveals his mind's content,—frank bias and honest prejudices. High authority in attaching the name of Marriage Group to the stories of only four of the pilgrims has doubly misled us, I think: first, by deliberately excluding from the debate on the moot questions of sex sovereignty and women's counsels several weighty disputants; and secondly, by disregarding copious indictments and defenses of other phases of matrimony. The theme of conjugal mastery is sounded not by the Wife₄ of Bath, but by Chaucer himself in his Tale of Melibœus, where the husband promises to obey Dame Prudence's wise counsels. Yet this full accord to the will of the woman is directly rebutted by the Monk's and Priest's examples of the deadliness of woman's advice. So begins a battle, which is concluded only by the Parson's insistence upon wifely obedience and loyalty. Four other phases of the woman problem beguile the pilgrimage, which often seems under the auspices of

Saint Venus rather than of St. Thomas:
—1) celibacy, 2) "gentilesse," 3) jealousy
4) contrast between good and bad wives.
1) Celibates like the Monk and his sort
should marry, says the Host, and beget
a worthy race. The Nun's Priest's Chan-
ticleer, the Cock, with his seven wives,
is the true precursor of the Wife of Bath
and her five husbands. The Wife's
heretical views of maidenhood are offset
by the chastity of Virginia and of Cecilia
(the old contrast of Venus and Virgin).
2) So under the text of "gentilesse"
or courtly love, we hear that the gentle
lover must leave all pride and villainy,
and ever be courteous, humble, gay,
generous, constant. What are the conventional symptoms of love? Whom
shall the lover choose, how win her, how
keep her favor? Of such are the tales of
Knight, Squire, Franklin, gentlemen all.
3) Jealousy is diagnosed in the *fabliaux*
of the churls, Miller, Reeve, Manciple—
tales of wily women, rascally lovers,
thwarted husbands. These recall the
Duck's contention in the *Parliament of
Fowls:* "There are more stars in heaven

than a pair." 4) The constrast between good and bad women is emphasized in the juxtaposition of Dame Constance and the wife of the Shipman's Tale— one, pure wife and noble mother, the other, sordid and venal. All these elements meet and mingle in the contribution of the Wife of Bath, which, in the most probable arrangement of the tales, falls by accident or design in the exact center of the fragmentary collection, being the twelfth tale of twenty-four. She epitomizes all the views of her fellows upon the woman question. She ever pleads for the sovereignty of her sex, the subjection of man to woman's will. Her famous prologue is a satire on celibacy in which the unorthodox views of this later woman of Samaria are barbed by pointed refutation of the cursed books of learned misogamists. She, the vulgarian, tells a courtly tale and gives the largest expression to views of gentleness. Jealousy and her plots against her husbands fill her thoughts. She confesses herself barley-bread in contrast with pure wheat-seed, the ascetic ideal. Moreover, she bears an obvious likeness to the wayward wives of the Miller's and Shipman's Tales, and she vies in shrewishness with the Hostess of the Tabard Inn. We yield to this doughty champion of womanhood the last word—the vaunt of her hard-won victory over her fifth husband:—

"He yaf me al the brydel in myn hond
 To han the governance of hous and lond,
 And of his tonge and of his hond also,
 And made him brenne his book anon right tho.
 And when that I hadde geten unto me,
 By maistrie, al the soveraynetee,
 And that he seyde, 'myn owene trewe wyf,
 Do as thee lust the terme of al thy lyf,
 Keep thyn honour, and keep eek myn estaat'
 And after that day we hadden never debaat."

BIBLIOGRAPHICAL NOTE

I

MEDIEVAL delight in generalization, fostering a larger interest in class categories and in stock types than in individuals, and medieval discontent with society may be readily studied in the social satires of the French moralists paraphrased by Ch. V. Langlois, *La Vie en France au Moyen Age, d'après quelques moralistes du temps* (Paris, 1908), and, on English ground, in the poems of Geoffrey Chaucer and of his contemporaries, John Gower and William Langland. The blending of conventionalism and pessimism finds copious illustration in H. O. Taylor's *The Medieval Mind* (London, 1911), Book IV, "The Ideal and Actual Society," and in several chapters of J. Huizinga's important volume, *The Waning of the Middle Ages* (London, 1924). The traditions of medieval orders and estates are inventoried in the famous *Chess Book* of Jacobus de Cessolis,

Liber de Moribus Hominum et Officiis Nobilium (Kopke, Brandenburg, 1879, and Vetter, *Das Schachzabelbuch Kunrats von Ammenhausen*, Frauenfeld, 1902), accessible to English readers in William Caxton's version ("Verbatim Reprint of First Edition" by William E. A. Axon, London, 1883). Read in this connection H. J. R. Murray's *A History of Chess* (Oxford, 1913), Part II, Chap. IV, "The Moralities." Ideals of kingcraft, traceable to the ethical traditions of Aristotle, are written large in the *Policraticus* of John of Salisbury (C. C. I. Webb, Oxford, 1909), in the *De Regimine Principum* of Egidio Colonna (French version, edited by Molenaer, New York, 1899), in the *Secreta Secretorum* (Three English versions, edited by Steele, *Early English Text Society, Extra Series*, LXXIV), and in *The Regement of Princes* by Thomas Hoccleve (Furnival, *Early English Text Society, Extra Series*, LXXII). The qualities of "the perfect knight" are the theme of Leon Gautier's magnificent work, *La Chevalerie* (Paris, 1883) and of W. H. Schofield's pleasant lectures, *Chivalry in English Literature* (Harvard, 1912). In addition to the many citations in the text, the reader may turn for a discussion of the medieval physician to H. P. Cholmeley's *John of Gaddesden* (Oxford, 1912); and for pictures of life on an English estate to Miss Lamond's excellent edition (1890) of Walter of Henley's *Husbandry* and to Miss Davenport's scholarly monograph, *Economic Development of a Norfolk Manor* (1896). The lecturer has drawn here and there from several articles of his own: "The Fall of Princes" (*The Nation*, April 5, 1919); "Chaucer's Doctour of Physik" (*The Nation*, June 26, 1913); and "The Quarrels of the Canterbury Pilgrims" (*Journal of English and Germanic Philology*, April, 1915).

II

The history of the medieval convention of the Seven Deadly Sins and the function of this formal sequence in the ecclesiastical scheme of things have been discussed by Lea, *History of Auricular*

Confession and Indulgences in the Latin Church, vol. II, and by Moore, *Studies in Dante, Second Series* (Oxford, 1899). Literary adaptation of the formula of the Vices may be studied in the *Purgatorio* of Dante, in the *Ancren Riwle* (modernized by Morton in *The King's Classics*), and in the passages of Langland, Gower, Dunbar and Spenser cited in the text of the lecture. For the use of the sequence in the drama of the Middle Ages consult W. R. Mackenzie, *The English Moralities from the Point of View of Allegory* (Boston, 1914); in religious songs F. A. Patterson, *The Middle English Penitential Lyric* (New York, 1911); in anecdotes, J. A. Mosher, *The Exemplum in the Early Religious and Didactic Literature of England* (New York, 1911); and in romance, Anthoine de la Salle's *Petit Jehan de Saintré* (Paris, 1830) and John Gower's *Confessio Amantis* (Macaulay, Oxford, 1901–1902). To illustrate Chaucer's ironical association of sins and social types, the lecturer has freely used his articles upon "The Quarrels of the Canterbury Pilgrims" (*Journal*

of English and Germanic Philology, April,
1915), "The Pardoner's Tavern" (*Id.*,
October, 1914) and "Chaucer's Sinners
and Sins" (*Id.*, January, 1916).

III

Among easily accessible medieval phi-
lippics against women and marriage are
*The Dissuasion of Ruffinus from Matri-
mony* of Walter Map (translated by Tup-
per and Ogle, *Courtiers' Trifles*, London,
1924), *The Seven Sages of Rome* (Killis
Campbell, Boston, 1907) and *The Romance of the Rose* (Englished by F. S.
Ellis, *Temple Classics*). For Christine
de Pisan's defense of her sex, see her
L'Epître au Dieu d'Amours (*Œuvres Po-
etiques de Christine de Pisan*, II, 1–27,
Societié des Anciens Textes Français,
1891), adapted by Thomas Hoccleve,
The Letter of Cupid (*Early English Text
Society, Extra Series. LXI*), and the
essay on the famous fifteenth century
feministe by Alice Kemp-Welch, *Of Six
Medieval Women* (London, 1913), which
includes Constance Fletcher's version of

Christine's greeting to Joan of Arc. The degradation of women in the *fabliaux* is discussed by Joseph Bédier in his critical study of those verse-tales (Paris, 1895) and in his chapter in Petit de Julleville, *Histoire de la Langue et de la Littérature Française*, vol. II, chap. 2 (Paris, 1896). Woman in medieval romance has been studied by Leon Gautier in his chapter on "Le Mariage du Chevalier" in *La Chevalerie*, by Ch. V. Langlois, *La Societé Française au XIII ͤ Siècle, d'après dix romans d'aventure*, Paris, 1911, and by Sarah F. Barrow, *The Medieval Society Romances* (New York, 1924). The conventions of courtly love are codified by Andreas Capellanus, *De Amore* (Trojel, Copenhagen, 1892), illustrated in the *Eric and Enid* and other romances of Chrétien de Troyes (translated with introduction by W. W. Comfort, *Everyman's Library*) and analyzed by L. F. Mott, *The System of Courtly Love* (Boston, 1896), W. A. Neilson, *The Origins and Sources of the Court of Love* (Harvard, 1899), W. G. Dodd, *Courtly Love in Chaucer and Gower* (Boston, 1913), and Miss

Barrow (cited above). The deification of woman by medieval mysticism is everywhere present in *The Early Italian Poets together with Dante's Vita Nuova* (translated by Dante Gabriel Rossetti). The woman of reality appears on *The Book of the Knight of La Tour-Landry* (English version in *Early English Text Society, Original Series*, XXXIII, 1906) and in *Le Ménagier de Paris* (Pichon, Paris, 1846), which has already been paraphrased by the lecturer in an article on "The Medieval Husband" (*The Sewanee Review*, XXVII, 1919, 330–342). All phases of the woman problem are aired by the Canterbury pilgrims and all meet and mingle in the prologue and tale of the Wife of Bath.